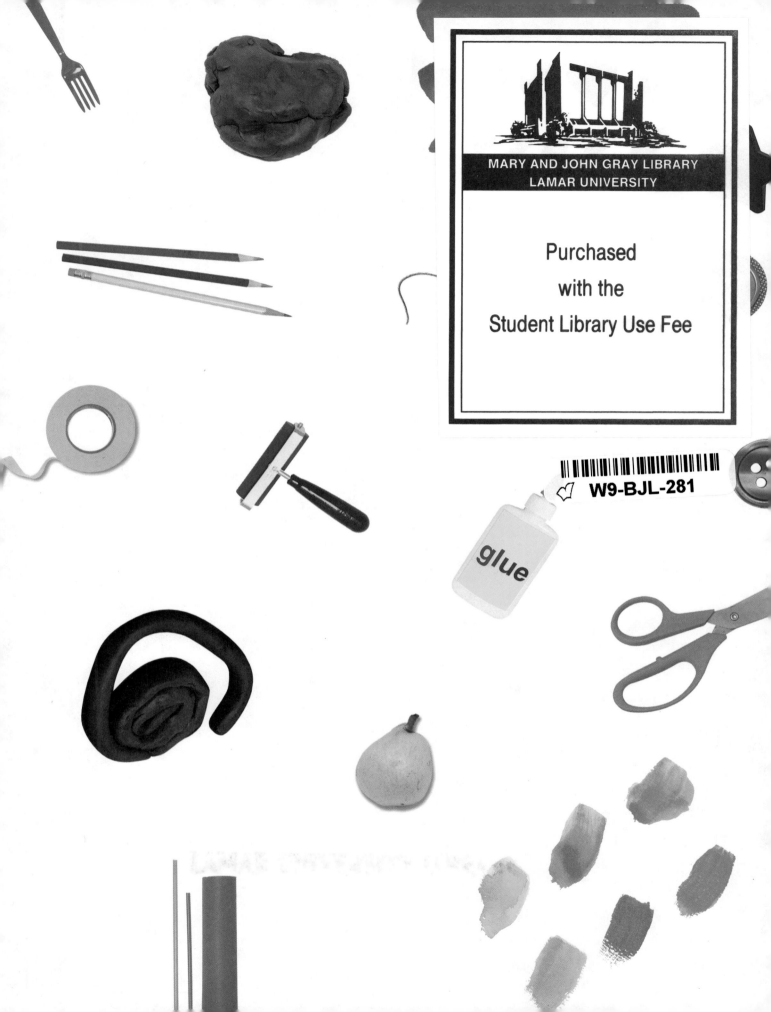

ART

Express

AUTHORS

Vesta A. H. Daniel

Lee Hanson

Kristen Pederson Marstaller

Susana R. Monteverde

Harcourt Brace & Company

Orlando   Atlanta   Austin   Boston   San Francisco   Chicago   Dallas   New York   Toronto   London

http://www.hbschool.com

ISBN 0-15-309316-1

3 4 5 6 7 8 9 10 048 2000 99 98

Dear Students,

What does the word *artist* mean to you? You may think an artist is someone who draws or paints. But photographers, weavers, and sculptors are also artists. Do you think of yourself as an artist?

The first artwork was made in prehistoric times by artists who painted on cave walls. Art materials, methods, and styles may have changed since then, but the reasons for making art have not. Artists today still create art to record history, communicate thoughts and ideas, and show beauty.

In this book, you'll see art from all over the world and from many different time periods. As you learn about these artworks and the artists who created them, you will get a chance to create your own masterpieces. You will draw a comic strip, make a diorama, and even carve a sculpture. Along the way, you may discover a new artist—you!

Sincerely,

The Authors

CONTENTS

 **UNIT 1** **Beauty All Around** ●14

 **UNIT 2** # Picturing People • 34

UNIT 3 · Expressions •54

UNIT 4

Reflections • 74

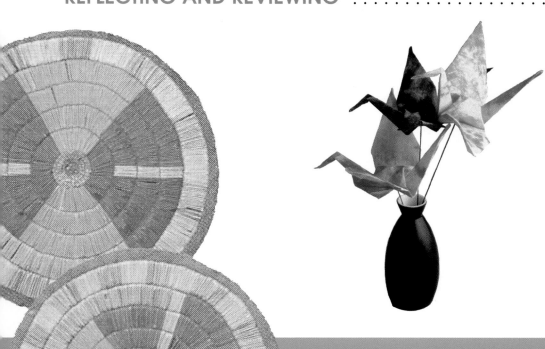

UNIT 5 **Inspirations** ●94

LOOKING AT ART

You may have seen art in a museum or in a book. Do you remember some artworks better than others?

You may want to follow these steps when you look at a piece of art. They will help you see the most important parts of the art.

1 **Look closely** at the art. What do you see? Take some time to describe it.

2 **How do your eyes** move around the art? What part of the art do you notice first? Think about why.

3 **Look at what** is happening in the art. What do you think the artist is trying to tell you?

4 **What do you think** of this piece of art? Discuss your thoughts with others.

Wherever you see art, take the time to really look at it.

KEEPING A
SKETCHBOOK

Fim Lynne Cherry

A **sketch** is a quick, simple drawing. Many artists draw sketches and write notes about their artwork in a **sketchbook**. Artist Lynne Cherry first made sketches of a snake and tree before completing this painting from *The Great Kapok Tree*.

These sketches and notes are from a student's sketchbook.

Bootsie sleeping

My Family

Here are some ways to use your sketchbook:

- **Plan your artworks.**
- **Record ideas for future projects.**
- **Write your thoughts about other people's art.**
- **Show what you see around you as an artist.**

YOU, too, can keep an art sketchbook. Choose a notebook that is large enough to draw in. (Unlined paper works best.) If you wish, you can decorate the cover. Then start filling the pages with your ideas, notes, and drawings.

Tomatoes and Fall Trees, **Janet Fish**
Oil on canvas, 1988. 48 X 60 in. Private collection.

Beauty All Around

How does an artist show the beauty found in natural and human-made environments?

Artists through time have chosen both natural and human-made environments as themes for their art. Nearly every culture has made art that shows the beauty found all around us.

In this unit you will see many ways in which artists show things created by nature and by people. Some artists focus on the smallest details of a single object. Others show wide views of the great outdoors.

ABOUT JANET FISH

Janet Fish creates lifelike paintings that show how light can add beauty to ordinary things. She often combines in her paintings items that would not normally be seen together.

Rock Art

Why do you think people made rock art and cave paintings?

Even before people used paper and pencil, they created pictures. Pictures **A** and **C** are **petroglyphs**. They were carved or scratched on rocks. Picture **B** was painted on the wall of a cave. No one knows who made these pictures, but you can tell that the artists knew these animals well. Name the animal you see in each picture.

Turtle
About 8 in. Cook's Peak,
Pony Hills, NM.

Rhinoceros
About 30,000 years
BEFORE PRESENT.
Chauvet Cave.
Ardèche Valley, France.

The turtle and the rattlesnake were found in the southwestern United States. The rhinoceros was painted on the wall of a cave in France. Trace with your finger the strong black **outline** that forms the shape of the rhino. The artist must have watched rhinos many times to know how to draw one so well.

 Rattlesnake
About 16 in. Cook's Peak, Pony Hills, NM.

IN THE STUDIO

MATERIALS

- **brown butcher paper or paper bags**
- **watercolors**
- **paintbrushes**
- **charcoal or soft pencils**
- **oil pastels or chalk**

Make a rock art drawing of an animal you are familiar with. Show what the animal is like.

1. **Lightly sketch your animal on a piece of brown paper. Make your sketch large.**

2. **Crumple the paper and smooth it out. Then brush the paper with water and add a gray or brown water-color wash.**

3. **Trace over the outline of the animal with a soft pencil or charcoal. Then add colors with oil pastels or chalk.**

Artful Regions

What kind of region is the setting for each painting? How can you tell?

Every region in the world is different. Artists show what a region is like by painting what they see there. What do you see in these paintings that helps you know what each region is like? Which region would you most like to visit?

Pictures **A**, **B**, and **C** are called **landscapes**. Artists paint landscapes to show very large areas.

 High Plains, **Thomas Hart Benton**
1953. Oil on canvas mounted on panel, 19 X 26 1/2 in.
Collection of the artist.

The part of a painting that looks closest to you is called the **foreground**. Where do you think the **background** is in a painting? How did these artists make the background look farther away than the foreground?

Compare the size of the mountains to the size of the tree in picture C. The artist painted the mountains much smaller than the tree to show that they are very far away. Notice that objects in the foreground are placed lower in each painting than those in the background. Where do you think the **middle ground** is in each painting?

Wooded Winter Landscape, Mortaratsch, Peder Monsted
Oil on canvas.

Cap d'Antibes, Claude Monet
Oil on canvas. Courtauld Institute & Galleries, London, England.

IN THE STUDIO

MATERIALS

- drawing paper
- colored pencils or oil pastels

Draw a landscape.

Make sure a viewer can tell what is close and what is far away. Draw objects in the foreground larger than objects in the middle ground or the background.

Visiting a Museum

An art museum brings together the works of artists from many places and times. Many cities and towns across the United States have art museums.

Some museums have docents [DOH•suhnts] to guide visitors through them. Docents give visitors information about the museum, the special exhibits, the artworks, and the artists.

Rose Bustamonte is a docent at the San Antonio Museum of Art. She used to be an art teacher. Now she passes on what she knows to some of the 27,000 students who visit the museum each year.

When you visit an art museum, don't rush through to try to see everything. Take time to look closely at some of the artworks. Ask yourself what an artist might have

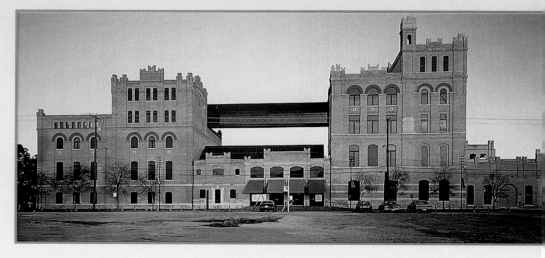

▲

San Antonio Museum of Art

been thinking as he or she worked. Choose a favorite artist or artwork to tell a friend or family member about.

You may notice that museum visitors walk slowly and speak quietly. They never touch the art. They are following the rules about how to behave in a museum. Why do you think museums have rules about keeping food and drinks out of the exhibit areas? What are some other rules that visitors should follow?

As a docent, Rose Bustamonte helps students learn about art.

WHAT DO **YOU** THINK ?

▶ **Look at the works of art in this book. Which ones would you like to see if you could tour the museums where they are kept?**

▶ **Why do you think it is important to have art museums?**

An Artist's Favorite Mountain

Why might an artist paint many pictures of the same place?

 Mont Sainte-Victoire, Paul Cézanne
1885–95. Oil on canvas. 28 5/8 X 38 1/8 in. The Barnes Foundation, Merion, PA.

These paintings show two views of Paul Cézanne's [say•ZAHN] favorite subject, a mountain near his home in France. Compare the sizes of the houses in picture **A.** Notice how the houses that are in the background look smaller than those in the foreground. **Proportion** is the size of one thing compared with the size of another. In this painting Cézanne used proportion to make things in the background look far away.

In picture **B**, the artist painted the mountain while standing in a different place. From this **point of view**, the mountain looks closer. Do you think Cézanne was standing nearer to the mountain when he painted picture A or picture B? Why?

In both paintings, Cézanne used simple shapes and bold colors to create powerful pictures of the mountain's beauty and size. Find some of the shapes he used.

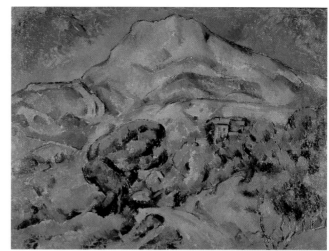

***Montagne Sainte-Victoire,*
Paul Cézanne**
Museum of Modern Western Art,
Moscow, Russia.

IN THE STUDIO

MATERIALS

- **watercolors**
- **paintbrushes**
- **thick paper**

From two different points of view, paint a place you know well.

1. **Think of a favorite place near where you live. Then think of two spots where you could get two different points of view of the place.**

2. **In your sketchbook, sketch the two views. Use proportion to show where objects are in the painting. Remember that objects in the background look smaller than those in the foreground.**

3. **Use your sketches as a guide to draw the two views on your paper. Use watercolors to paint the two views.**

Nature's Shapes

What do you think these artists wanted you to notice about these objects?

Sometimes artists use different methods to help us see natural objects in new ways. They may do this by using close-up views and unusual shapes and colors.

Look at pictures **A** and **B**. Notice the close-up view of leaves in picture A. The rounded, uneven shapes of the leaves are called **organic** shapes. Organic shapes are like those found in nature. How are organic shapes different from other shapes you have seen?

Notice that the red leaf in the bottom right corner of picture A is a lighter red than the leaves behind it. These two reds are different in **value**. Value means how light or dark a color looks.

Autumn Leaves, Lake George, N.Y.,
Georgia O'Keeffe
1924. Oil on canvas, 20 1/4 X 16 1/4 in.
Columbus Museum of Art, Columbus, OH.

24

The artist has used colors with different values to make some of the leaves stand out.

Now look at the dark wave and the white spray in picture B. The **contrast** between these two colors makes the wave stand out. Does the wave look threatening? Why?

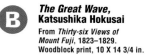

B ***The Great Wave,*** **Katsushika Hokusai**
From *Thirty-six Views of Mount Fuji,* 1823–1829.
Woodblock print, 10 X 14 3/4 in.

IN THE STUDIO

MATERIALS

- charcoal or soft pencils
- drawing paper

Draw a close-up.

Find an object that is interesting to look at. Draw a close-up view of it. Use contrast and value to make details stand out.

Seeing Designs in Nature

What do you think these photographs show? Crepe paper? A new style of art? Actually, they are pictures of rock formations in Arizona.

The lumpy land shown to the right is Navajo sandstone. The wavy rock shown below is from a slot canyon, a type of canyon that is narrow and deep. Wind and rain caused these designs to form in the rock surfaces. What do you think is interesting in these pictures?

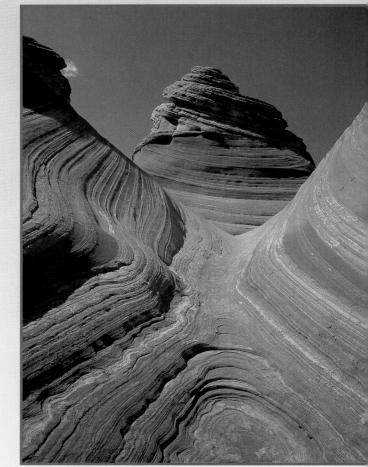

▲ Navajo sandstone

◀ Slot canyon

You don't have to go to Arizona to find eye-catching shapes and patterns. Is there anything familiar about these pictures? These close-up views show the interesting patterns on the surfaces of a pineapple and a strawberry.

Many natural objects seem like works of art in themselves!

pineapple

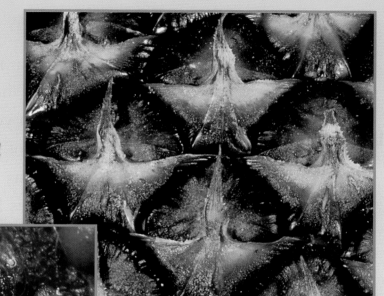

strawberry

WHAT
DO
YOU
THINK
?

▶ **What designs have you seen in nature? Describe them.**

▶ **If you wanted to turn one of these designs into a work of art, what materials would you use?**

Natural Scenes

How have the artists made these animals look at home?

Mount Equinox, Winter, **Rockwell Kent**
1921. Oil on canvas,
34 1/8 X 44 1/4 in.
The Art Institute of Chicago,
Chicago.

The place where an animal lives is its environment. Each of these pictures shows an animal in its natural environment. How can you tell that the animals in pictures **A** and **B** do not live in the same place?

Notice how the artists used space to show what each animal's environment is like. The artist who painted picture A has shown us the wide-open spaces where the deer lives. The mountain sits far in the distance. This environment is very different from the bird's home in the tree branch in picture B.

Another way of showing an animal in its environment is by making a **diorama**. A diorama shows space by placing figures in front of a painted background.

 Magnolia Flowers with Bird, **Tchcou Tsien-Tsieou**
18th–19th century, China. Watercolor.
Musée Cernuschi, Paris, France.

IN THE STUDIO

MATERIALS

- **shoe box and lid**
- **scissors**
- **tempera paints**
- **paintbrushes**
- **twigs, grass clippings, small rocks, sand**
- **glue**

Make a diorama that shows an animal from your region in its natural environment.

1. **Cut out one of the long sides of a shoe box. On the box lid, draw the animal you have chosen. Draw a tab on the bottom of your animal. Cut the animal out and fold the tab back.**

2. **Paint the inside of your box to look like your animal's environment.**

3. **Glue your animal and natural objects from your region into your box.**

Still Lifes

What catches your eye most in each picture?

Each of these paintings is a **still life**. A still life is a picture of an arrangement of objects. A still life usually shows an indoor setting.

Artists arrange objects in a still life in different ways. Sometimes all the objects overlap, as they do in picture **A**. Sometimes the artist also leaves space between objects, as in picture **B**. Why do you think an artist would choose one way over another?

Look for details in the paintings. Did you notice any part of picture A that stood out?

 Still Life of Flowers, **Rachel Ruysch**
1689. Oil on canvas, 26 1/2 X 21 3/4 in. Private collection.

The part of a painting that stands out is called the **center of interest**. Artists use a center of interest to show **emphasis,** or importance. What is the center of interest in picture A?

B

Still Life with Three Puppies, **Paul Gauguin**
1888. Oil on wood, 36 1/8 X 24 5/8 in. The Museum of Modern Art, New York.

IN THE STUDIO

MATERIALS

- **tempera paints**
- **thick paper**
- **paintbrushes**

Paint your own still life. Decide how to place the objects to make an interesting arrangement.

1. Place three or more objects on a table. Decide whether or not the objects will overlap. Move the objects around until you like the arrangement.

2. Sketch the still life lightly in pencil on your paper.

3. Paint your still life with tempera paints.

Artists see the beauty all around us.

From prehistoric times to today, artists have created art
to show the beauty found in nature. Artists have also
found beauty and interest in the world of people.

Thunderstorm in the Rocky Mountains,
Albert Bierstadt
1859. Oil on canvas, 19 X 29 in.
Museum of Fine Arts, Boston.

What Did I Learn?

- **LOOK** back at your artwork in this unit. Think about what you did to show depth and distance. In which piece did you best show depth and distance? Explain how you did it.

- **EXPLAIN** why you think some artists choose not to show depth and distance in their paintings.

- **LOOK** at the painting on page 32. *Thunderstorm in the Rocky Mountains* was painted by Albert Bierstadt. Many people think that he was a very great painter of landscapes. Do you agree or disagree? Explain your reasons.

- **FIND** an artwork that you like in this unit. Explain why you chose it. Then tell how it is like *Thunderstorm in the Rocky Mountains* and how it is different.

Paul as Harlequin, **Pablo Picasso**
1924. Musée Picasso, Paris.

Picturing People

Some artists paint lifelike portraits. Others make sculptures of people or paint portraits that look very unusual. Some artists show one person. Others show groups of people. How would you describe the portrait on page 34?

In this unit, you will see many of the ways artists show people.

In what ways do artists show people?

ABOUT PABLO PICASSO

Pablo Picasso [PAH•bloh pih•KAH•soh] was a very well-known artist of the 1900s. He created paintings, sculptures, drawings, prints, and ceramics.

Portraits

Why do you think artists paint portraits?

Pictures **A** and **B** are **portraits**. An artist paints a portrait to show how a person looks or what a person is like. What can you tell about the people in these portraits? How are they alike? How are they different?

Notice the proportion of the features on each face. You know that proportion is the size of one thing compared with the size of another. Each person's eyes are about halfway between the top of his head and his chin. The tip of the nose is halfway between the eyebrows and the bottom of the chin. The lower lip is halfway between the tip of the nose and the bottom of the chin.

Portrait of a Boy (also known as *Portrait of the Artist's Son Titus*), **Rembrandt van Rijn**
About 1645–50. Oil on canvas, 25 1/2 X 22 in. The Norton Simon Foundation, Pasadena, CA.

Contour lines are the lines around the edges, or the outlines, of a shape or form. Both heads are oval. But the subjects look very different from each other. How did each artist make his subject look unique?

B *Stephen Austin,* **artist unknown**
Archives Division, Texas State Library.

IN THE STUDIO

MATERIALS

- **colored pencils or crayons**
- **white paper**

Draw a portrait of an adult.

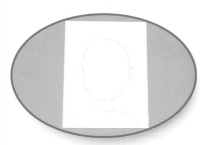

1. Use a pencil to lightly sketch the contour lines of the person's head.

2. Look at the shapes of the person's eyes, nose, and mouth. Sketch them onto the portrait. Keep in mind what you learned about proportion.

3. Add details such as hair and clothing. Then add color to your sketch.

Relief Sculptures

How can an artist show what someone looks like without using pencils, paints, colors, or paper?

Look carefully at pictures **A**, **B**, and **C**. How are they alike? Do you think they could be called portraits? Why or why not?

These pictures show **relief sculptures**. Each image has been carved from a surface so that it stands out from the background. Some relief sculptures, like the one in picture A, are huge. These 60-foot-high faces were carved into a mountain. Coins, like the one in picture B, are tiny relief sculptures.

A *Mount Rushmore National Memorial, Gutzon Borglum*
1927–41. Granite.
Black Hills of South Dakota.

Pictures B and C each show a **profile**, or side view, of a person. In picture C, the sculptor carved lines to show the soft texture of the woman's hair and dress. What other details do you notice in this sculpture?

IN THE STUDIO

MATERIALS

- clay
- butter knife
- carving tools (pencil point, paper clips)

Carve a relief sculpture of a friend.

1. Sketch a friend's profile.

2. Roll out a slab of clay. Trim the edges with a butter knife to form a shape for the background.

3. Use your sketch to help you carve the profile in the clay. Use a pencil point or one end of an opened paper clip. Press and carve the clay to show your friend's features.

FORMAL PORTRAITS

Have you ever noticed that no matter what people look like every day, they want to get all dressed up for their family portraits?

For centuries, people have been dressing up and posing to say "cheese." Long ago, only rich people had their pictures made, and they wanted to look as fine as possible. The portrait by Diego Velázquez on page 41 is a typical portrait of a wealthy European.

Family portrait About 1890–95. Newfoundland, PA.

◀ **Student school picture**

Some portraits from the past didn't even look like the people who sat for them!

The painter George Catlin got tired of this style. He admired the ways of the American Indian so greatly that he painted many pictures to record their culture. What does the portrait below tell you about how Catlin felt about White Cloud?

Today we use photographs to record special times and to remember the people who mean the most to us. This shows that friends and family are important in our culture.

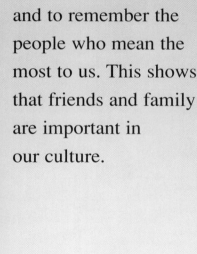

Equestrian Portrait of Elizabeth of France,
Diego Velázquez
About 1635. Oil on canvas, 301 X 314 cm. Museo del Prado, Madrid, Spain.

The White Cloud,
Head Chief of the Iowas, **George Catlin**
1844–45. Oil on canvas, 27 3/4 X 22 3/4 in. National Gallery of Art, Washington, D.C.

WHAT DO **YOU** THINK ?

► **What can you tell about these people from their portraits?**

► **Describe the kind of portrait you would like to have made of yourself.**

Abstract Portraits

How are these paintings like and unlike other portraits you have seen?

Pictures **A** and **B** are both portraits of the same girl. Notice the details that the artist showed in picture B. A real princess posed for this portrait. Now find the same details in picture A. This portrait was painted 300 years later. The artist used picture B as his model. Look at the straight lines, large shapes, and bold colors. Can you find a yellow cube and some blue triangles?

Picture A is an **abstract** portrait. The painter of an abstract portrait often uses unusual colors and shapes. This shows the subject in a way that is different from real life.

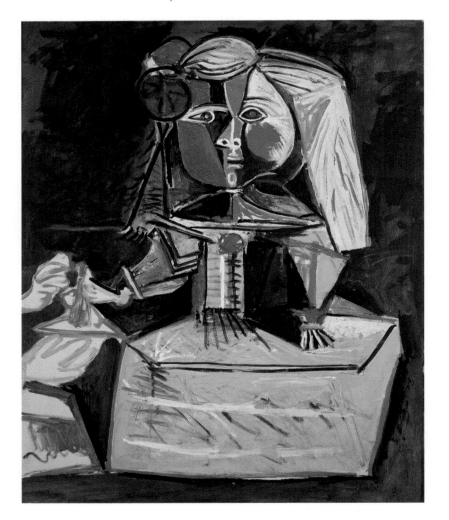

The Infanta, **Pablo Picasso**
1957. Oil on canvas, 31 3/4 X 36 in.
Museo Picasso, Barcelona, Spain.

IN THE STUDIO

MATERIALS

- colored markers (primary and secondary colors)
- white construction paper

Use unusual colors and shapes to draw an abstract portrait.

1. Fold your paper in half the long way. Unfold it. Then fold it in thirds to form six boxes.

2. Sketch a person's forehead, hair, and eyes in the top two boxes. Use straight lines and interesting shapes.

3. In the middle boxes, draw the cheeks, ears, and nose. Draw the mouth, chin, and neck at the bottom. Use bright colors to finish your portrait.

Shades and Tints

How does color show mood in a painting?

Look at the people in these paintings. Which group seems happier? Does the color in each painting make you feel a certain way? Sometimes artists use warm colors like red and yellow to create a cheerful mood. Cool colors such as blue and green can make us feel lonely or sad.

A

Poor People on the Seashore (The Tragedy), Pablo Picasso

1903. Oil on wood, 105.4 X 69 cm. National Gallery of Art, Washington, D.C.

Artists may use one main color to set a mood. What is the main color in picture **A**? In picture **B**? A picture with one color is said to be **monochromatic**.

How do artists make a color darker or lighter? They add black to create darker values called **shades**. They add white to create lighter values called **tints**.

 El Pan Nuestro, Diego Rivera
Education Secretariat, Mexico.

IN THE STUDIO

MATERIALS

- **paintbrushes**
- **tempera paints**
- **paper plate**
- **white paper**

Paint a picture of people. Use color to show a mood.

1. **Decide whom you would like to paint. What will the people be doing? Think of the mood you want to show in your painting. Which color shows this mood best?**

2. **Add different amounts of black and white paint to the color you chose to create shades and tints.**

3. **Paint the people, using the monochromatic color scheme you have chosen.**

John Steptoe Paints a Story

Have you ever seen birds like these? Who might the three people on the next page be? Both of these pictures are illustrations from John Steptoe's book **Mufaro's Beautiful Daughters,** *which retells an African folktale.*

In this picture, the artist used cool colors to show the rich beauty of the African land. The other picture is a portrait of Mufaro and his daughters. What can you tell about each person?

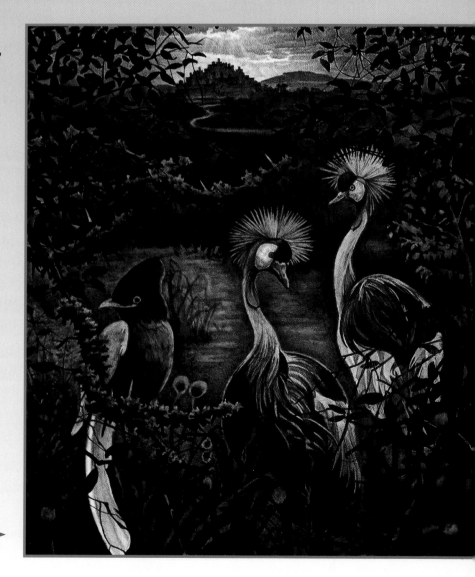

African birds ▶

46

John Steptoe wrote and illustrated his first book when he was sixteen years old. During his lifetime, he wrote and illustrated many award-winning books.

▲ **Manyara, Mufaro, and Nyasha**

WHAT
DO
YOU
THINK
?

▶ **Would you like to meet the characters in this folktale? Why might they be interesting?**

▶ **How did John Steptoe show depth in the African landscape?**

Rhythm and Unity

What can an artist show by painting a group of people rather than a portrait?

Pictures **A**, **B**, and **C** show groups of people doing things together. What are the people doing in each painting? What story does each painting tell?

Artists tie the parts of a painting together to give it **unity**. They may do this by repeating colors or shapes. What image is repeated in picture A? José Clemente Orozco [oh•ROHS•koh] painted many yellow sombreros to show unity.

 Zapatistas, José Clemente Orozco
1931. Oil on canvas, 45 X 55 in. The Museum of Modern Art, New York.

Blue Dancers,
Edgar Degas
Hermitage Museum,
St. Petersburg, Russia.

Freedom March,
Anna Belle Lee Washington
Oil on canvas.

Look at the curves and colors in picture B. The artist, Edgar Degas [duh•GAH], repeated them to give his painting a sense of **rhythm**. Can you imagine how the dancers are moving? Look for examples of rhythm and unity in picture C.

IN THE STUDIO

MATERIALS	Draw a group of people in action.
• crayons • drawing paper	Repeat an image in your picture to create rhythm and unity.

People in Motion

How did these artists show that their subjects were moving?

Artists sometimes paint portraits. At other times they paint people in motion. What are the people in pictures **A** and **B** doing? How can you tell they are in motion?

 Munich Olympic Games, **Jacob Lawrence**
1971. Gouache on paper, 35 1/2 X 27 in.

 Snap the Whip **(detail), Winslow Homer**
1872. Oil on canvas, 12 X 20 in.
The Metropolitan Museum of Art, New York.

Artists use action lines to create a sense of **movement**. In paintings that show action, the subjects often slant to the right or left. Artists create this look with **diagonal lines**. What are the main diagonal lines in pictures A and B? The artist who painted picture **C** used horizontal lines of different lengths to show movement. How would you change picture C to show the man and woman sitting in a parked car?

C

In the Car, Roy Lichtenstein
1963. Magna on canvas, 67 3/4 X 80 1/8 in.
Scottish National Gallery of Modern Art,
Edinburgh, Scotland.

IN THE STUDIO

MATERIALS

- **soft black pencil**
- **oil pastels**
- **drawing paper**

Use diagonal and horizontal lines to draw people in motion.

1. In your sketchbook, sketch a group of people in motion. Decide where to use action lines to show movement. When you are satisfied, draw your picture on white paper.

2. Color your picture with oil pastels. Try to make the action lines stand out.

Artists sometimes create art to show the many sides of people.

They may show people alone or in groups, sitting still or in motion. Their art celebrates people and their stories.

School's Out, Allan Rohan Crite
1936. Oil on canvas, 30 1/4 X 36 1/8 in.
National Museum of American Art,
Smithsonian Institution, Washington, D.C.

What Did I Learn?

- **THINK** about how you used proportion in your drawings of people. What did you find most difficult about this technique?

- **LOOK** back through the artworks in this unit to find examples of profiles. What similarities and differences do you see in the profiles? Why might an artist choose to show a profile instead of a front view of a person?

- **USE** clues in the painting on page 52, called *School's Out,* to tell a story about what is happening. What are the people doing in the painting? Where do you see examples of movement?

- **FIND** another picture in this unit that shows three or more people together. What similarities and differences do you notice between that picture and the one shown here?

Sketch for *Howl*.

***Howl*, Luis Jiménez**
1986. Cast bronze, 60 X 29 X 29 in.
Collection of the artist.

Expressions

How might

a piece of

art express,

or show,

the artist's

feelings

about

something?

Sometimes artists use their art to express their feelings. How might art be better than words for showing how you feel about something?

As you look at the art in this unit, think about what the artists might be trying to express. What feelings might the artist be trying to show in *this* work?

ABOUT LUIS JIMÉNEZ

Luis Jiménez [hee•MAY•nes] believes that American art should represent the many cultures that have helped build the United States. Much of his work focuses on his Mexican heritage.

Animal Sculptures

What do you think was happening just before each of these horses and riders was "frozen in time"?

Since ancient times, horses have served people as workers, transportation, and friends. These pictures show horses doing some of these jobs. Picture **A** shows a cowboy taming a wild horse to be a work animal. The horse in picture **B** also carries a cowboy. Compare this horse with the horse in picture A. In picture **C**, a musician rides a horse in a royal parade. How do you think these artists felt about horses?

Notice how the horses in pictures A and B seem to be in motion. The horse and rider in picture C seem still and proud. The figures in pictures A, B, and C are **sculptures**. A sculpture is a **three-dimensional** form. It has height, width, and depth, and it can be viewed from many sides.

A   *The Bronco Buster,*
Frederic Remington
Modeled 1894–95, cast about 1907.
Bronze, 22 in. with base.

B
Vaquero, Luis Jiménez
1977. Molded fiberglass, 16 ft. 6 in. x 24 ft. 9 in. x 5 ft. 6 in.
Moody Park, Houston.

C
Painted pottery horseman,
unknown Chinese artist
Tang Dynasty (A.D. 618–907). Pottery.

IN THE STUDIO

MATERIALS	Mold a clay animal sculpture.
• modeling clay	Show your animal at work. Include a person to
• toothpicks	show how people and animals work together.

Comic Strips

What is the message of this comic strip?

Peanuts comic strip, **Charles M. Schulz** January 7, 1990. © 1990 United Feature Syndicate, Inc.

Comic strips can make us laugh. But they can also show an artist's ideas or opinions. This comic strip makes us think about how we feel when we compare ourselves to others. How do you think this artist wants us to feel about ourselves?

An artist who creates comic strips is called a **cartoonist**. The characters that a cartoonist creates belong to the artist. How does a cartoonist show how a character is feeling? The dog in this comic strip is Snoopy. The lines in Snoopy's face can make him look surprised, worried, proud, or bored. The lines above Snoopy's paws in the first frame show movement. A cartoonist can tell a story with a few simple lines.

IN THE STUDIO

MATERIALS

- **colored pencils**
- **drawing paper**

Make up your own characters and create a comic strip.

1. Think of a message you could tell in a comic strip.

2. Make up one or two characters for your comic strip. Practice drawing them in your sketchbook until you get a picture you like.

3. Decide how many frames you'll need to tell your story. Write the words your characters will say in each frame. Then draw the characters and color them.

ANIMATOR

There's something almost magical about animated shows. The characters seem so real! Who brings these drawings to life? Animators like Chuck Jones do.

An animator, like any artist, shows a viewpoint through his work. Chuck Jones shows Bugs Bunny as confident and witty. Bugs seems ready to face any situation. Daffy Duck is his jealous sidekick. How do you think Chuck Jones showed these characters' personalities in his work?

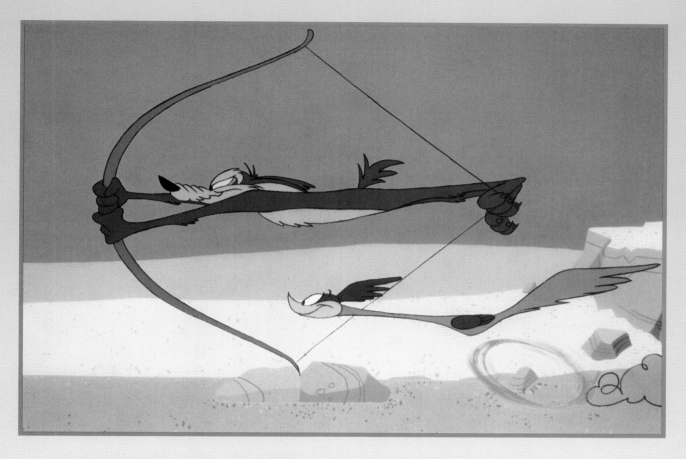

In 1996, at the annual Academy Awards ceremony, Chuck Jones won the Lifetime Achievement Award for his work. He has been animating the famous Warner Brothers cartoon characters since 1934. For over sixty years, children and adults have been delighted by the comical situations these characters have faced.

WHAT DO **YOU** THINK ?

▶ **What animated characters are your favorites? What do you like about them?**

▶ **How can you see the personalities of these characters from the way they are drawn?**

Important Symbols

How can colors and shapes be used to show what is important to people?

Look at the pictures on these pages. Do you recognize any of them? Each one contains **symbols** that stand for things or ideas that are important to people. The eagle, for example, is a symbol that stands for freedom. What do you think some of the other symbols in these pictures stand for?

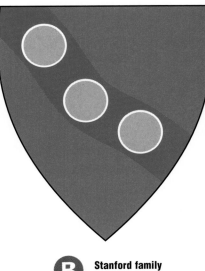

B Stanford family coat of arms

Pictures **A** and **B** show **coats of arms**. Coats of arms were first used about 800 years ago. They were painted on knights' shields so their soldiers would recognize them in battle. Later they were used to represent families. Picture B identifies the Stanford family. The name *Stanford* comes from "stone ford." This is a place where a river can be crossed on stepping stones. Find the symbols for stones, a river, and a green field in picture B.

A Great Seal of the United States

Pictures **C** and **D** show state seals. The symbols in each one tell about the history of the state.

C Seal of the state of Texas (reverse side)

D Edmund G. Brown building with the California state seal

IN THE STUDIO

MATERIALS

- paintbrushes
- tempera paints
- cardboard
- scissors

Create a coat of arms with symbols of things that are important to you.

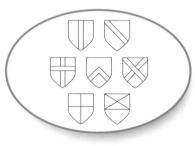

1. **Draw a large shield on a piece of cardboard. Cut it out. Divide your shield into sections. These are common ways to divide shields.**

2. **Draw a symbol inside each section. Each symbol should stand for something important to you, such as a pet or a favorite sport or hobby.**

3. **Paint your coat of arms.**

Common Products as Art

What makes

these pictures

works of art?

When is a soup can a work of art? When an artist helps us see it that way. Would a soup can be art if it were in a grocery store? A common object can become art when it is used in a new way. The art shown here is called Pop Art. How do pictures **A** and **B** help us see common objects in a new way?

Andy Warhol painted pictures A and B to look like prints. To make a **print**, an artist creates one picture on a stamp or stencil. The artist can then use the stamp or

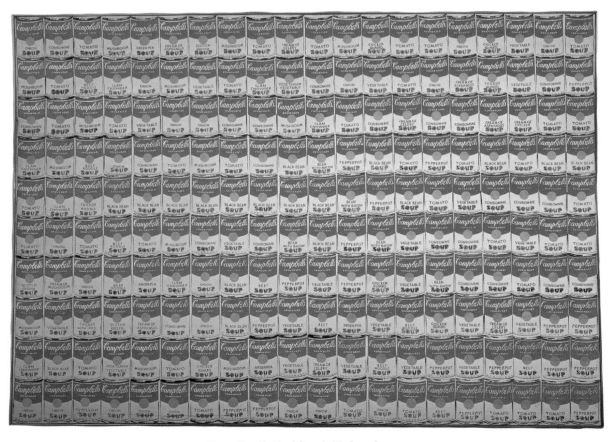

 Two Hundred Campbell's Soup Cans,
Andy Warhol
1962. Synthetic polymer paint on canvas, 72 X 100 in.
Private collection.

stencil to make many copies of the picture.

These pictures show hundreds of objects that are almost exactly the same. What do you think the artist is telling us about the world we live in?

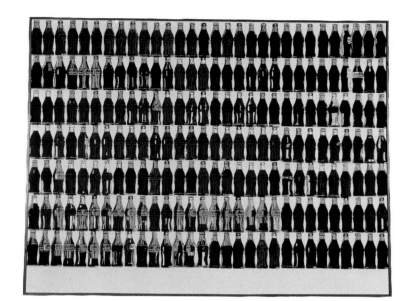

210 Coca-Cola Bottles, **Andy Warhol**
1962. Synthetic polymer paint and silkscreen on canvas.
6 ft. 10 1/2 in. X 8 ft. 9 in. Private Collection.

IN THE STUDIO

MATERIALS

- **foam food trays**
- **cardboard**
- **newspapers**
- **scissors**
- **water-base printing ink or thick paint**
- **brayer**
- **white paper**
- **tape**

Create prints that show an everyday object as art.

1. **Think of an object that has a simple shape. Draw the shape on a foam tray, and cut it out. Then tape a folded strip of cardboard to the back of your shape to make a handle.**

2. **Use a brayer to apply an even layer of ink or paint on the front of your shape.**

3. **Create an interesting pattern by repeating your shape many times on a piece of paper. Be sure to press down on the entire back of the shape.**

Lynne Cherry's World

Chances are, you've read lots of books that tell about the world around you. But have you ever read one written from the point of view of an armadillo? In **The Armadillo from Amarillo,** *by Lynne Cherry, Sasparillo the armadillo wants to know more about his place in the world.*

Lynne Cherry is an award-winning author and illustrator. She often draws and writes about the natural world. In this book, Lynne Cherry's paintings show us the different environments Sasparillo visits—including outer space! One of these paintings is a cityscape. Imagine that you are next to Sasparillo, looking down from the tower. What can you see below you?

▲
Lynne Cherry

To make her paintings look real, Lynne Cherry visited many different places and took pictures of them. She also looked at postcards, magazines, maps, photographs, and even computer-made pictures of earth as seen from space! Lynne Cherry says, "Art is a wonderful way to express the beauty I see in life."

▲ **Sasparillo looks down at the city from a high tower**

WHAT DO YOU THINK ?

► **Why do you think Lynne Cherry used a cityscape to show Sasparillo's first visit to a city?**

► **What places would you like to see? Why?**

Cityscapes

What idea of city life does each painting show?

Each of these paintings is a **cityscape**, or a scene from a city. How is a cityscape different from a landscape? How do you think each artist felt about city life?

Notice how each artist used light. In picture **C**, light seems

 Windows, **Charles Sheeler**
1951. Oil on canvas, 32 X 20 1/8 in. Hirschl and Adler Galleries Inc., New York.

 Sidewalk Cafe at Night, **Vincent van Gogh**
1888. Oil on canvas. Kröller-Müller Foundation, Otterloo, The Netherlands.

to come from deep inside the building. In picture **A**, the bright light comes from the sun. The light in picture **B** comes from inside the buildings. It spreads a soft glow through the whole scene. How does the light affect the mood of each cityscape?

What shapes do you see in these pictures? Compare the shapes you see in pictures A and C with those in picture B. Imagine that you could walk into one of these paintings. Which one would you choose? Why?

 Radiator Building, Georgia O'Keeffe
1927. Oil on canvas, 48 X 30 in. Fisk University, Nashville.

IN THE STUDIO

MATERIALS

- **black or brown crayon**
- **white paper**
- **white-glue-and-water mixture**
- **tissue paper (various colors)**
- **thick paintbrush**

Make a cityscape that expresses a mood.

1. **Use a crayon to make a line drawing of a cityscape. Show your idea of city life. If you have not visited a city, draw what you think city life is like from things you have seen or read.**

2. **Brush the glue-and-water mixture over your drawing.**

3. **Press layers of tissue paper onto parts of your drawing. Use different colors to create a mood.**

Artistic Styles

A *Untitled,* **Tom Lochray** Computer-generated art

How are these pictures alike? How are they different?

Look at the cloud of smoke coming from the train in each picture. The smoke in picture **A** looks like round bubbles. In picture **B** the smoke cloud is shown as light and shadow. What does the smoke look like in picture **C**?

These paintings show differences in **style**. Style is the way an artist chooses to show a subject. In a **realistic** painting, the objects look like things in the real

B *Gare Saint-Lazare, Paris, (The Railroad Station),* **Claude Monet** 1877. Oil on canvas, 32 1/4 X 39 3/4 in. Fogg Art Museum, Harvard University, Cambridge, MA.

world. Which painting is realistic? The style of picture B is **Impressionistic**. The artist showed his idea, or "impression," of how the light was reflecting off the surfaces. Picture A is **stylized**. The artist left out details to show things as simple shapes.

Which style of painting do you like best? Why?

IN THE STUDIO

MATERIALS

- **2 sheets of white paper**
- **oil pastels**
- **colored markers**
- **scissors**
- **glue**

Try this new style to make a picture of a train.

1. **Use colored markers to draw a picture of a train. Leave the background blank.**

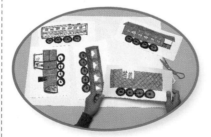

2. **Cut your drawing into five pieces. Spread the pieces out on a large piece of paper. Turn and separate the pieces to change the image. Glue them onto the paper.**

3. **Use markers to connect the parts of the train. Draw an interesting background with oil pastels.**

Art is a way for artists to express their viewpoints.

Sometimes a piece of art clearly shows an artist's opinion. At other times, viewers must look closely for clues to what the artist thinks, feels, or believes.

Goldfish Bowl II, Roy Lichtenstein
1978. Painted bronze, 29 X 25 1/4 X 11 1/4 in.
Edition of three.

What Did I Learn?

- **THINK** about the symbols and colors you used in your art to show what is important to you. What other clues in your art show how you feel about something?

- **LOOK** at the sculpture on page 72. The artist used bright colors and made his art look flat. He made a three-dimensional object look two-dimensional. How do you think he solved this problem?

- **THINK** about the art you have seen in this unit. Which piece do you think most clearly shows the artist's opinion about something? What do you think the artist's opinion is?

Jar, María Martínez and Julian Martínez
1934–43. Matte black-on-black earthenware, 10 5/8 X 13 5/16 in.
The Museum of Fine Arts, Houston.

Reflections

How do

pieces of art

show the

cultures in

which they

were

created?

Look at the details on this jar. Can you tell where it was made? The feathers at the top and the snake around the middle are traditional images of the American Southwest.

Many pieces of art provide clues about the cultures in which they were created. As you look at the art in this unit, watch for clues that tell what culture each piece came from.

ABOUT MARÍA MARTÍNEZ

María Martínez helped bring the ancient art of Native American black-on-black pottery into the twentieth century. She and her husband developed techniques and styles based on ancient models.

Marvelous Masks

What do you think these masks may have been used for?

A ***Mask,***
Sargent Johnson
1933. Copper,
10 7/8 X 7 7/8 X 2 3/8 in.
San Francisco Museum
of Modern Art.

Think about the last time you wore a mask. Why did you wear it? Masks have been used by nearly every group of people over time for many different purposes. Performers may wear ceremonial masks to tell stories. These masks are often made to look like people or animals.

76

Picture **A** shows a copper mask. It has features that are similar to the masks made in Africa since early times. The mask has a **variety** of textures. What do you think the hair feels like? What about the forehead?

Picture **B** shows a Mexican jaguar mask. For hundreds of years jaguars have appeared in the art of Mexico. The ancient Mayas of Mexico thought the jaguar was a symbol of strength and courage. In a traditional Mexican dance, you might see a dancer playing the part of a jaguar.

B **Jaguar mask**
About 1960. Painted wood, 9 1/2 in. Mexico.

IN THE STUDIO

MATERIALS

- tagboard (about 7 x 11 in.)
- paper scraps
- scissors
- glue
- fibers (straw or yarn)
- colored markers
- hole punch
- elastic (8 x 1/4 in.)

Create a mask of your favorite story character.

1. **Draw an outline of the character's face on the tagboard and cut it out.**

2. **Cut out holes for the eyes and the mouth. Fold, bend, and curl paper scraps to make the nose, ears, and other features. Glue them to the mask. Glue on fibers for hair or fur. Use markers to add details.**

3. **Punch a hole on each side of the mask. Tie on the elastic. Try on your mask.**

Paper Shapes

How can artists create art from paper without using pencils, pens, or paints?

Artists in China and Poland cut these rooster shapes from paper. In many cultures, the rooster is a symbol of new beginnings. Why do you think this is so?

Look at the rooster in picture **A**. The red shapes themselves are called **positive shapes**. The empty space around the positive shapes creates **negative shapes**. Point to the positive and negative shapes in picture A. How did the artist use negative shapes to show details?

A **Rooster**
About 1960. Cut paper, 4 1/4 X 4 in.
Northern China.

Now look at the rooster in picture **B**. You can see the outlines of the rooster's feet. They are called **actual** lines. Trace them with your finger. Notice how the feet overlap the grass. You cannot see the outlines of the grass behind the feet, but you know the grass is there. The hidden outlines are **implied** lines. Look for examples of implied lines in magazines, signs, and posters.

B **Rooster,**
Marianna Pietrzak
1962. Cut paper,
8 3/4 X 6 3/4 in.
Bledów Lowicz, Poland.

IN THE STUDIO

MATERIALS

- **construction paper—black and another color**
- **scissors**
- **glue**
- **black marker**

Make a cut-paper shape of your favorite animal.

1. Draw the outline of your animal on a sheet of colored paper. Make the animal as large as you can.

2. Cut out the animal. Trim the edges to make details such as fur or feathers.

3. Glue your animal onto the black paper. Use a marker to draw more details.

CONNECTIONS ART AND CULTURE

ORIGAMI

Have you ever folded a paper hat or made a paper airplane? In some cultures, paper folding called **origami** *[awr•uh•GAH•mee] is an art form.*

Paper folding probably started in China before the sixth century. At that time the folded paper objects were used in ceremonies. Today in Japan, the tradition of origami is passed from one generation to the next. Children learn basic paper folds in school. Some of Japan's artists produce fantastic creations from paper.

▲
One traditional paper fold is the crane.

There are all kinds of origami, from decorative packages to unusual shapes. Some are animals, like the koala bear, the peacocks, and the crane. Next time you are in the library, look for books about origami. Then try your hand at it!

▲

The directions for making these peacocks include 42 different steps.

This koala is made from one piece of paper.

▼

WHAT DO **YOU** THINK ?

► **What kinds of objects would you like to see as origami?**

► **Can you think of other examples of traditional art? Describe what the art is like.**

Pottery

What do these objects show us about the people who made them?

These pieces of **pottery** are made of clay. For thousands of years, people have made **vessels** like these to hold water and other things. How do you think these vessels were made?

The bowl in picture **A** was made by a Pueblo Indian **potter** in New Mexico. After the bowl was formed, it was baked in a hot oven called a **kiln**. Baking makes the clay hard. Pottery is often decorated with images that have special meaning. What does the design on the bowl remind you of? The potter puts this bear paw shape on many of her works. It is a Pueblo symbol for water.

 Bowl, Margaret Tafoya
About 1984. Carved and polished earthenware, 7 1/2 X 14 in. Museum of International Folk Art, Museum of New Mexico, Santa Fe.

Notice the graceful designs and bright blue color on the old Vietnamese jar in picture **B**. The Vietnamese potter used a special dye called cobalt to create such a deep blue color.

 Jar, unknown Vietnamese potter
Le dynasty, mid-15th century. High-fired stoneware with underglaze cobalt-blue decoration. 26.5 cm. Museum of Fine Arts, Boston.

In the Studio

MATERIALS

- clay
- slip (clay mixed with water)
- rolling pin
- plastic knives, old pencils, toothpicks

Make a clay coil pot. Decorate it in a special way.

1. **Flatten some clay with a rolling pin. Cut out a circle for the base of your pot.**

2. **Make long ropes by rolling clay on a flat surface. Lay a clay rope along the outer edge of your base. Coil another rope on top of it. Wet the outside edges with slip and press them together.**

3. **Continue adding coils until you like your pot's shape. Smooth the walls. Scratch designs on the sides.**

Radial Balance

How are these objects alike?

Put your finger on the center of the web in picture **C**. Notice how the web's pattern fans out from the center. Now do the same with the objects in pictures **A** and **B**. What do you notice about their patterns? When a circular design is arranged around a center, it has **radial balance**.

Radial balance can be found in some natural objects, such as the spiderweb. Human-made objects can also show radial balance. Native Americans of the southwestern plains made the **ornaments** shown in pictures A and B to decorate their tepees. The circle is an important symbol for the Plains Indians. It is a symbol of how everything in the world is connected.

A Sioux tepee ornament
About 1920–30. Colter Bay
Visitor Center, Grand Teton
National Park, WY.

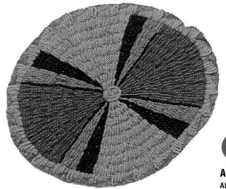

B Arapaho tepee ornament
About 1875–1900. Colter Bay Visitor
Center, Grand Teton National Park, WY.

Notice the different colors and patterns. The ornament in picture A was made by a Sioux [SOO] artist. The one in picture B was made by an Arapaho [uh•ROP•uh•hoh] artist.

Spiderweb

IN THE STUDIO

MATERIALS

- **wire circle loom**
- **yarn**
- **large, blunt needlepoint needle**
- **beads, feathers, other ornaments**

Make a circle weaving that shows radial balance.

1. **Draw a few large circles in your sketchbook. In the circles, sketch simple designs for your weaving. Choose the one you like best.**

2. **Tie ten pieces of yarn across the loom as shown. Pinch the pieces together at the center. Tie them together with another piece of yarn. Tie the end of this piece to the loom.**

3. **Thread a needle with yarn. Weave yarn over and under, around the loom. Use different colors to create the design you sketched. Decorate your weaving with ornaments.**

FIREWORKS

Fireworks displays are such a big part of American culture that the Fourth of July wouldn't be the same without them. But did you know that people in China have been enjoying fireworks since the tenth century? After a cook made a mixture that gave off sparks, people packed the ingredients into bamboo "rockets." They were shot into the sky to create colorful explosions.

The Chinese used fireworks to celebrate weddings, victories, and the New Year. The first fireworks were shades of yellow and red. It wasn't until the mid-1800s that a way was found to create green, white, and blue.

Over the years, fireworks have become bigger and better. Some fireworks shows are combined with music and special effects. Have you ever seen an amazing fireworks show?

In the United States, fireworks displays have become a traditional part of New Year's Eve and Fourth of July celebrations. Many places are known for putting on spectacular fireworks shows. Some popular places are the Mall in Washington, D.C., New York City, and large theme parks.

WHAT DO YOU THINK ?

▶ What's the most exciting fireworks display you have ever seen? What made it so good?

▶ How are fireworks today different from fireworks in the past? How are they the same?

Styles of Architecture

Where do people who design buildings get their ideas?

These buildings are all located in the United States. Yet each one has a very different style of **architecture**, or building design. How are these buildings different from one another?

Notice the curved lines of the arches and the dome-shaped roof in picture **A**. This style of architecture was brought to the U.S. by people from Spain. Now look at the Japanese Tea House in picture **B**. What is the first thing you notice about the building? Roofs that curve up at the ends were first made in China. Later they were used in Japan.

What does the building in picture **C** remind you of? Trace your finger along the **pyramid** form. This form was used in ancient Egypt.

A San José Mission
Completed in 1720.
San Antonio, TX.

 Japanese Tea House and Garden,
George T. Marsh
Completed in 1894. San Francisco, CA.

 Transamerica Tower,
William Pereira & Associates
Completed in 1972. San Francisco, CA.

In The Studio

MATERIALS

- **cardboard**
- **tagboard**
- **cardboard scraps**
- **markers or crayons**
- **scissors**
- **glue**

Create a model of the front of a building. Make your model show a style of architecture.

1. **Decide what style your building will have. You might choose from the styles shown on these pages.**

2. **On cardboard, draw an outline of the front of the building. Then cut it out.**

3. **Add details by cutting shapes from tagboard. Glue them to the front of the building. Show depth by gluing cardboard scraps between the cardboard and the tagboard.**

Puppets

What kinds of stories could be told with these puppets?

These figures are **puppets**. How do you think they work? The puppet shown in picture **A** is a **marionette**. It is moved by strings that are tied to different parts of its body. The puppet is from a marionette theater in Austria. It is one of the characters in a famous opera called *The Magic Flute*.

A

Marionette of Papageno
Wood, fabric, feathers, and paint.
Salzburg Marionette Theatre,
Austria.

The puppet in picture **B** is a **shadow puppet**. Which of its parts move? How can you tell? This kind of puppet is held up behind a thin screen. Light shines on the screen from behind the puppet, and its shadow moves. Shadow puppets are popular in many parts of Asia. This one is from China.

B **Shadow puppet, artist unknown**
19th century. Cut, painted leather, 20 1/4 in. China.

IN THE STUDIO

MATERIALS

- **cardboard**
- **paper fasteners**
- **scissors**
- **craft sticks**
- **paper clips**
- **tape**
- **tempera paints**
- **paintbrush**

Make a shadow puppet with arms you can move.

1. **Sketch the outline of a person on paper, and cut it out. Cut each arm into two pieces.**

2. **Trace the shapes onto cardboard. Draw a tab at the top of each arm piece. Cut out the pieces. Use paper fasteners to attach the arms at the tabs.**

3. **Tape a craft stick to the back of your puppet. Tape a straightened paper clip to each hand. Practice using these wires to move your puppet's arms. Paint your puppet.**

Artists can use their art to show beauty and to tell about their culture, time, and place.

The art in this unit helped you better understand the history and traditions of several different cultures.

Texas Peaceable Kingdom,
Becky Crouch Patterson
1986. Appliquéd stitchery, 5 X 6 ft.
Collection of the artist.

What Did I Learn?

- **THINK** about the art you created in this unit. How did you use patterns in your artwork? What kinds of patterns did you use?

- **LOOK** at the art shown on page 92. What clues do you see that tell you the art came from the American Southwest? Point out some examples of implied lines.

- **FIND** a piece of art from this unit that you especially like. What do you like about it? What can you tell about the culture it came from?

Gandhi, Margaret Bourke-White
1946. Gelatin silver print, 11 X 14 in. *Life* magazine © Time Warner.

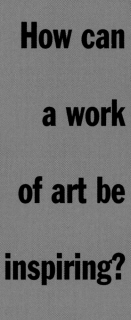

How can a work of art be inspiring?

Inspirations

Have you ever seen a piece of art that you thought was especially beautiful in some way? Did it inspire you to do something? Did it make you feel good? That is what some art is meant to do.

Why might some people find this picture inspiring? The man in the picture was a spiritual and political leader of the 1900s who helped free India from British rule.

ABOUT MARGARET BOURKE-WHITE

Margaret Bourke-White became interested in photography at a young age. She traveled the world to photograph important people, places, and events.

95

Photographic Point of View

How can a photographer change the way we look at the world?

Photography is the art of taking pictures. Photographers can make things look dramatic or inspiring by taking pictures from new points of view. Look at the redwood trees in picture **A**. This picture was taken from the ground looking up, showing us a **worm's-eye** point of view. A worm's-eye view makes us see how huge the redwoods are.

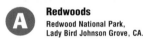
A **Redwoods**
Redwood National Park,
Lady Bird Johnson Grove, CA.

Picture **B** shows a **bird's-eye** view of the Statue of Liberty. Where do you think the photographer was when she took this picture? How would the statue look if the photographer had used a worm's-eye view?

B *Statue of Liberty,* **Margaret Bourke-White**
Date unknown. Silver-gelatin print, 19 3/16 X 15 7/16 in.
Art Institute of Chicago.

Picture **C** shows Dr. Martin Luther King, Jr. The photographer took this picture at eye level. Why do you think the photographer did not choose a bird's-eye view? Why do you think photographers take pictures from different points of view?

Dr. Martin Luther King, Jr., **Flip Schulke**

IN THE STUDIO

Make a photomontage, using pictures that show different points of view.

1. **Choose a large picture for the background of your montage. Glue the picture to the poster board.**

2. **Practice placing smaller pictures with different points of view over the background to create an interesting effect.**

3. **Cut out parts of the smaller pictures that you want to use in your montage. Glue them to the background.**

Memorials for Heroes

How can artists help us remember heroes?

The sculptures in pictures **A** and **B** are **memorials**. Memorials remind us of people or events. Notice how different the memorials are. One is made of huge stone blocks. The other shows a relief sculpture.

The memorial in picture A honors police officers who died. The artist wanted to create a special place by using the land. He formed a pyramid out of the ground. The memorial is almost as big as a football field.

The memorial in picture B honors African American soldiers who fought in the Civil War. The sculptor used real people as models, so each face is different.

Houston Police Officers Memorial, Jesús Bautista Moroles
1992. Granite and earth. Houston, TX.

To create a large artwork such as a memorial, an artist first makes a scale model, called a **maquette**. It helps the artist plan the artwork.

 Robert Gould Shaw Memorial (overall view and detail), Augustus Saint-Gaudens
1884–96. Bronze, 11 X 14 ft. Boston Common, Boston.

IN THE STUDIO

MATERIALS

- squares of cardboard
- cardboard tubes
- different kinds of paper
- drinking straws
- tape or glue
- scissors

Design a maquette of a memorial.

1. Sketch a picture of a three-dimensional memorial to honor someone you admire. Include geometric shapes in the design.

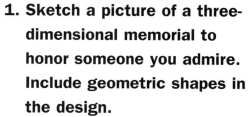

2. Create forms out of paper and other materials. Tape pieces of paper together to form cones, cubes, or other shapes.

3. Tape or glue the forms to a cardboard base to complete your memorial. Write a sentence or two describing the person it honors.

Say It with Pictures

Some people in large cities have found a way to bring a little bit of nature into their lives. They have started community gardens in vacant lots or wherever space is available.

You can learn more about community gardens in the book *Greening the City Streets: The Story of Community Gardens.* Author Barbara Huff and photographer Peter Ziebel take readers on a tour of several gardens in New York City. Ziebel's colorful photographs help readers understand the author's discussion of community gardens by giving visual examples. They show how community gardens add a bit of beauty to crowded city neighborhoods.

▲ This garden has a sunflower-growing contest, with prizes for both the widest and the tallest flowers.

Clinton Community Garden has a parklike lawn and many garden plots. The members also keep bees to make honey. ▶

By summer, the plants escape their plot borders and take over the garden.
▼

WHAT DO **YOU** THINK ?

▶ **What do Peter Ziebel's photographs tell you about the gardens and the community?**

▶ **Imagine you have designed a project to improve your community. What kind of pictures would best show your ideas?**

101

Murals

Why might artists create paintings on the walls of public buildings?

A **mural** is a painting done on a wall. A mural often tells a story or presents a message. What stories do you think the murals in pictures **A** and **B** tell?

Picture A shows a community mural in Houston, Texas. It was painted by a group of students. Why do you think the artists included flags from many countries?

 Community Mural
East End neighborhood, Houston, TX.

JEWISH ARTS & SCIENCE

Picture B shows part of a mural in Los Angeles, California. The entire mural is almost half a mile long. It is the biggest mural in the world. The artist wanted to show that people of different backgrounds are valuable to the community. Hundreds of people from the Los Angeles area worked on the mural.

 B *The Great Wall of Los Angeles,* (detail) **Judith Baca** 1976–83. Tujunga Wash, Studio City, CA.

IN THE STUDIO

MATERIALS

- rolls of butcher paper
- tempera paint
- paintbrushes

Work with classmates to create a mural.
Your mural should present a message you want to share. Sketch your mural first. Make sure each part sends a clear message. Then paint the mural.

Landscaped Gardens

How can a garden also be a work of art?

Some artists turn natural settings into works of art. They use living plants and other objects to create artistic gardens for people to enjoy.

 Garden at Blenheim Palace, Sir John Vanbrugh
1705–22. Woodstock, England.

 Garden of the Adachi Museum, Nakane Kinsaku
Honshu, Japan.

104

Look at pictures **A** and **B**. These are landscaped gardens—they have been carefully designed and cared for.

The garden in picture A has **symmetrical balance**. Each side of the central water garden is a mirror image of the other side. Shrubs are trimmed to form exact shapes. Objects are evenly spaced.

The Japanese garden in picture B is outside a museum. People view the garden through a window that looks like a picture frame. The garden's design has **asymmetrical balance**. The plants and rocks have different sizes and shapes. They are grouped together in a varied pattern. What else makes this garden asymmetrical?

IN THE STUDIO

MATERIALS

- colored paper, fabric, foil, string, sand
- large sheet of paper
- scissors
- glue

Use mixed materials to make a design for a garden.

1. **Think about the kind of garden you would like to make. Sketch a symmetrical or an asymmetrical design.**

2. **Cut out fabric, foil, or paper shapes to match the shapes in your design.**

3. **Glue the shapes onto your design. Then glue sand where you want it.**

Park Designer

A designer is an artist who plans how something will look. Designers work in hundreds of different jobs. Some plan books; others plan billboards. Some designers plan places in the community.

Norma Beasley is a designer who usually works on books. One day, Norma's neighbors asked her to help design a community park.

Before Norma could begin designing the park, she had to ask many questions. Who would use the park? How would they use it? How could costs be kept low?

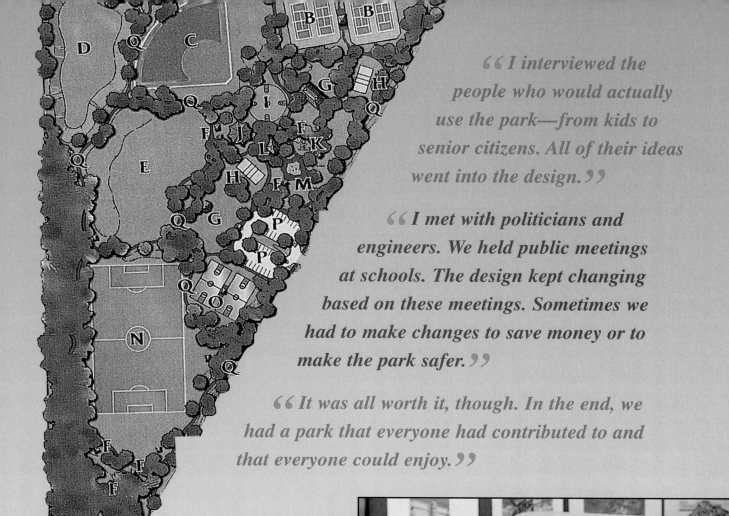

> *I interviewed the people who would actually use the park—from kids to senior citizens. All of their ideas went into the design.*

> *I met with politicians and engineers. We held public meetings at schools. The design kept changing based on these meetings. Sometimes we had to make changes to save money or to make the park safer.*

> *It was all worth it, though. In the end, we had a park that everyone had contributed to and that everyone could enjoy.*

WHAT DO YOU THINK?

▶ How is designing a public place, like a park, different from designing a private place, like a yard?

▶ If you could design a park, what special features might you include? Why?

Historical Buildings

How can buildings preserve history?

Look at the buildings in pictures **A** and **B**. Each was built as a place of worship. What do you find most beautiful about each one? Picture A shows a **cathedral** [kuh•THEE•druhl] in France. Construction of this building took nearly 100 years. Notice the two rectangular towers at one end and the large round window in the middle.

Notre Dame Cathedral
12th century. Paris.

The building in picture B is a **mosque** [MOSK] in Turkey. Its roof includes many domes of different sizes. Four tall towers, called minarets, stand at its corners. They seem to pierce the sky. How does the design of each building make it inspiring?

These buildings are considered historical buildings. They can tell us much about the past. Each building is like a treasure to its country. What do these buildings tell us about the people who built them? Why might people want to preserve them for the future?

**The Blue Mosque,
Mehmet Aga**
1609–16. Istanbul.

IN THE STUDIO

MATERIALS

- drawing paper
- ruler
- colored pencils

Draw an imaginary building that may someday become historic.
Include architectural features and details in your design to make it inspiring.

Stained-Glass Windows

Why do you think stained-glass windows are used in important buildings?

This **stained-glass** window was made about 750 years ago for Notre Dame Cathedral in Paris. It is called a rose window because of its flowerlike shape. Many people think it is one of the most beautiful stained-glass

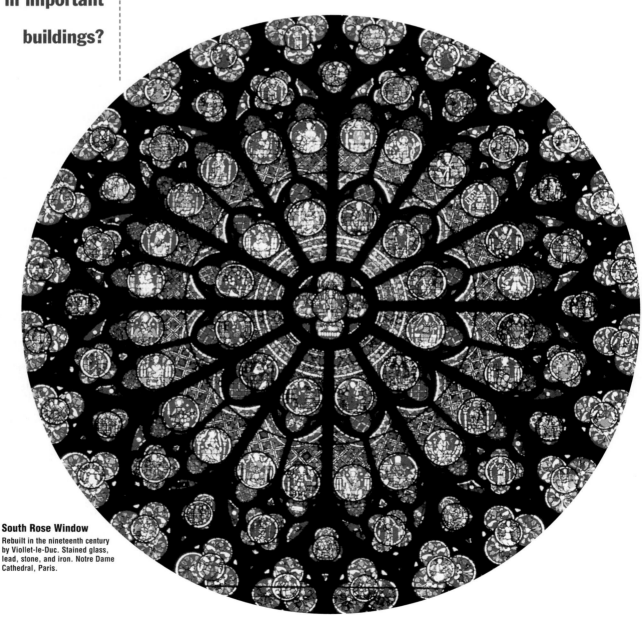

South Rose Window
Rebuilt in the nineteenth century by Viollet-le-Duc. Stained glass, lead, stone, and iron. Notre Dame Cathedral, Paris.

windows in the world. The window is made of thousands of pieces of colored glass.

In the Middle Ages, glassmakers found that adding metals to melted glass made brilliant colors. The colored glass is **translucent**—light can pass through it, but it blocks a view of objects on the other side. Strips of a soft metal called **lead** hold the small pieces of glass together. The thick lines are the window's stone frame. Notice the radial balance in the window. Trace your finger along lines that show radial balance.

South Rose Window (detail)

IN THE STUDIO

MATERIALS

- black construction paper
- colored tissue paper
- scissors
- large round lid
- tape

Design a rose window that has radial balance.

1. Use the lid to draw a large circle on black paper. Cut out the circle and fold it in half three times.

2. Cut shapes out of the folded sides of your circle. Make sure that you don't cut all the way across. Unfold the circle to show your design.

3. Tape pieces of tissue paper over the holes in your design. Now turn the circle over and hold it up to the light.

Some art inspires us to work for a better world.

In this unit you saw art such as gardens, buildings, and memorials that can't be found in a museum. These artworks add beauty to our communities.

The Lincoln Memorial in Washington, D.C.

What Did I Learn?

- **THINK** about some of the art you created in this unit, such as the memorial and the mural. What messages or ideas did you try to show through your art?

- **THINK** about what you learned about maquettes, or scale models. In what ways can maquettes help artists plan large works of art?

- **LOOK** at the memorial shown on page 112. Do you recognize it? It is the Lincoln Memorial in Washington, D.C. How might people feel inspired by this memorial?

- **LOOK** back through the art in this unit. Which piece do you find the most inspiring? Why?

Lever #1, Martin Puryear
1988. Red cedar, 167 1/2 X 132 3/4 X 17 3/4 in.
The Art Institute of Chicago.

Expect the Unexpected

What makes

something

a work

of art?

Artists sometimes challenge our ideas about what art is. They may use unusual materials or paint in unusual ways.

Look at the piece of art shown here. What is it? Sometimes artists create things that are simply meant to be enjoyed.

ABOUT MARTIN PURYEAR

Martin Puryear grew up in Washington, D.C. As a boy, he often visited the Smithsonian's Museum of Natural History, where he enjoyed sketching the exhibits. He later went to Africa and Sweden to learn more techniques for woodwork and sculpture.

Surrealist Art

How can artists make paintings look like scenes from dreams?

Can clocks and watches bend like cloth? Can people stand on air? They can in a **Surrealist** painting. Surrealist painters show the impossible and the unexpected in a reasonable way.

Have you ever had a dream in which something impossible seemed normal? Perhaps you were running at impossible speeds. Or breathing underwater. Whatever it was, you accepted it in the dream. These unreal ideas can be found in the works of Surrealist artists.

 Soft Watches, **Salvador Dalí**
1933. Oil on canvas, 81 X 100 cm. Private collection.

What is the center of interest in picture **A**? How did the artist make the picture look strange? What impossible scene has the artist shown in picture **B**?

Golconda, René Magritte
1953. Oil on canvas, 31 7/8 X 39 3/8 in.
Private collection.

IN THE STUDIO

MATERIALS

- drawing paper
- watercolors
- paintbrushes

Paint a Surrealist scene.

You may want to distort an ordinary object to make it look strange or show a scene that could not really happen.

Creating in Unusual Ways

Why do artists explore new ways of making art?

David Hockney made picture **A** by first molding paper pulp. This is the liquid form of paper. He dyed the pulp and used combs, brushes, and other household objects to give it texture. The thick pulp could be used to make simple shapes only. Hockney had to carefully plan how to show a pool with this material. How did he show the light sparkling on the water? What colors show shadow, light, and depth?

 Steps with Shadow (Paper Pool 2),
David Hockney
1978. Pressed color-paper pulp, 50 1/2 X 33 1/2 in.
Private collection.

To make picture **B**, Jackson Pollock stood over the canvas and dripped, spattered, or flung paint onto it. To make it seem full of movement, Pollock made long, looping trails of paint. These curved, continuous lines keep viewers' eyes moving through the painting. The many layers of paint create texture. How do you think the artist was feeling when he painted this?

B

No. 1, **Jackson Pollock**
1949. Enamel and metallic paint on canvas,
63 in. X 102 in.

IN THE STUDIO

MATERIALS

- **drawing paper**
- **thick paints**
- **objects with which to apply paint and to make textures**

Paint a picture using an unusual method or unusual materials. Use one or both of these methods, or invent your own.

Use common objects to make textures in paint.

Paint with unusual objects.

119

AUTO ART

Have you ever seen a car driving down the road that really caught your eye? Imagine what you'd see in an art car parade!

Car artists use automobiles to express their ideas. Some of the artists are making serious statements, but most are just having fun. In the United States you can see art cars at festivals and exhibits around the country.

▲ This "carmadillo" is built over a pickup truck wheelbase and a van frame.

One unusual group of autos can be found in an exhibit by the School of Visual Arts in New York. On display are old cars that have been recycled as works of art. Students at the school were asked to give these old cars a new purpose. Among their creations are a mouse-trap, an accordion, a toaster, a shower, a subway car, a movie theater, a submarine, a diner, and a fireplace! Which of the cars shown here is your favorite?

This telephone, barbecue grill, and grand piano are all made from old cars.

WHAT DO **YOU** THINK **?**

▶ Describe an art car you would like to create.

▶ Do you think people should be allowed to drive unusual art cars on the public streets? Why or why not?

A Balancing Act

How can an artist make a sculpture that moves?

Look at the sculptures in pictures **A** and **B**. How are they different from other sculptures you have seen? What might happen if you pulled on the black rectangular shape in picture A? What if you tapped the sculpture in picture B?

The moveable sculptures shown here are called **mobiles**. They were made by Alexander Calder. He was the first sculptor to create mobiles as a form of art. A mobile works like a seesaw. To stay in motion, the hanging parts must be balanced. What would happen if the parts were not balanced?

A ***Indian Feathers,* Alexander Calder**
1969. Painted sheet metal, rod, 11 ft. 4 3/4 in.
Whitney Museum of American Art, New York.

To make a mobile, Alexander Calder first cut out hundreds of different shapes. Then he arranged them in different ways until he liked what he saw.

 Lobster Trap and Fish Tail, Alexander Calder
1939. Painted steel wire and sheet aluminum, 8 1/2 X 9 1/2 ft. Museum of Modern Art, New York.

IN THE STUDIO

MATERIALS

- branches and twigs
- string or fishing line
- various found objects such as acorns, stones, shells, small toys

Create a mobile with moving parts that are balanced.

1. **Tie a piece of string to the middle of a thick branch. This will form the top part of your mobile.**

2. **Gather two or three twigs. Hang two or three objects from each twig. Be sure each twig is balanced when you hold it up with the string.**

3. **Tie the twigs to the top branch. To balance your mobile, you may need to adjust where each twig is tied to the branch.**

Unusual Forms

What do these sculptures remind you of?

These sculptures may remind different people of different things. The sculptures in pictures **A** and **B** are **nonrepresentational**. The artists did not try to make them look like, or represent, anything else.

 Texas Shield, **Jesús Bautista Moroles**
1986. Texas granite, 75 X 43 X 27 in.

What kind of shape does the sculpture in picture A have? Now notice the organic shape of the sculpture in picture B. It has a rounded, curving form. You can see through it to the other side. What kind of feeling does each sculpture give you?

 Hollow Form with White Interior, **Barbara Hepworth**
1963. Partially painted guarea wood, 39 in.

IN THE STUDIO

MATERIALS

- **instant papier-mâché or old newspapers and flour-and-water mixture**
- **tempera paints**
- **paintbrushes**

Create a papier-mâché sculpture that is nonrepresentational.

1. **Twist or wad up some newspaper into a simple shape. If you like, try leaving an open space in the shape. This will be the shape of your sculpture.**

2. **Apply layers of wet paper strips to your shape. Let each layer dry before adding the next.**

3. **Paint your sculpture.**

TOPIARY GARDEN

By now, you have seen paintings of landscapes. But did you know there is a landscape of a painting?

Artist James T. Mason created this topiary garden in downtown Columbus, Ohio. Topiary is the art of trimming and training shrubs into special shapes. Mason's garden is based on Georges Seurat's famous painting *A Sunday Afternoon on the Island of La Grande Jatte*. Visitors roaming around the garden feel as if they have walked into the painting!

A Sunday Afternoon on the Island of La Grande Jatte, **Georges Seurat**
1886. Oil on canvas, 6 ft 9 in. X 10 ft.
Art Institute of Chicago.

Mason's Topiary Garden is best viewed from a place overlooking the park. From this point, you can see the view shown in Seurat's painting.
▼

Mason spent months designing and forming the bronze frames that contain the plants. He and his wife began shaping and tying branches to the sculptures in 1989. The figures should be completely filled in by 1998. The Masons must take good care of the garden to protect it from freezing winters and summer droughts.

The tallest topiary character stands twelve feet high. It is so big that it took several people and some heavy equipment to put it up. There are fifty topiary characters in all. How do you think travelers passing through the city react to this sight?

Eight topiary boats are located in the pond. They include a steamboat, a sailboat, and a boat with four rowers.

WHAT DO YOU THINK ?

▶ **If you were creating a topiary garden, what objects would you show?**

▶ **Do you think Mason's garden might change the way some people feel about art? Explain your answer.**

Whimsical Sculpture

What kinds of materials can be used to make sculptures?

Not all sculptures are made from stone. Sculptors can use all sorts of materials. What materials were used to make the sculptures in pictures **A** and **B**?

Sculptures like these are whimsical. The artists thought of fanciful ways to use unusual materials. Sometimes the idea for a sculpture comes from the materials themselves.

Notice the sturdy materials used in the sculpture in picture A. What does the sculpture seem to say about working women? How do its materials help express this?

Working Woman, **Marisol**
1987. Wood, charcoal, and plaster,
96 1/2 X 28 X 20 in.
Sidney Janis Gallery, New York.

Look at the sculpture in picture B. The artist who made it said that he got his ideas as he worked with the wire. What part of an elephant do you think curved wire made him think of?

B *Elephant,* Alexander Calder
About 1930. Wire, 10 in.
Present location unknown.

IN THE STUDIO

MATERIALS

- **heavy aluminum foil**
- **scissors**
- **masking tape**
- **cardboard pieces**
- **stapler**
- **glue**

Create a whimsical animal sculpture.

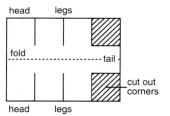

head   legs
fold ---------- tail
head   legs
cut out corners

1. **Cut your foil as shown.**

2. **Fold and crumple the foil to form your sculpture. Then bend the sculpture into an interesting pose.**

3. **Wrap tape around the foil. Staple or glue your finished sculpture to a piece of cardboard and display it.**

An Impossible Building

Why is this picture worth a second look?

Waterfall, **M. C. Escher**
1961. Lithograph, 14 7/8 X 11 3/4 in.
Cordon Art, Baarn, The Netherlands.

Look closely at this building. What is the water doing that could not really happen? If you said that it seems to flow uphill, you are right. The artist has tricked your eye by creating an **illusion**. Notice that both towers appear to be the same height. Yet one is three levels high, and the other is only two.

What other things in the picture don't make sense? Find some plants that look as if they could swallow a person whole. These plants would look normal if they were much smaller. The artist has changed their sizes to make them look strange.

M. C. Escher [EH•sher] is well known for artwork that tricks the eye. He studied to be an architect. However, he found that playing with shapes and space was more interesting.

In the Studio

MATERIALS	**Sketch an impossible building.**
• white paper • soft pencils or charcoal	Create an illusion that tricks the eye. Or draw a building that could not exist, such as a house made of ice on a warm tropical island.

In this unit you learned that artists can surprise us.

They may use unusual materials in their artwork. Or they may create a piece of art that challenges reality—they make the impossible look believable.

Flowers, Jim Love
1965. Steel and cast iron,
27 5/8 X 19 X 17 1/2 in.
The Menil Collection,
Houston.

What Did I Learn?

- **REVIEW** the art you created in this unit. Which art project did you enjoy most? What did you enjoy about it? What techniques did you use?

- **THINK** about the art that showed impossible scenes. Why do you think artists create art that shows something that could not really happen or exist?

- **LOOK** at the sculpture on page 132. What is surprising about it? How does it help you see everyday objects in a new way?

- **COMPARE** this sculpture to other pieces of art in this unit. How is it similar? How is it different? Which piece of art did you find the most surprising? Why?

ART SAFETY

Listen carefully when your teacher tells how to use art materials.

Wear a smock to keep your school clothes clean.

Use the kind of markers and inks **that will not stain your clothes.**

Use tools carefully. Hold sharp objects so that they cannot hurt you or others. Wear safety glasses if something could get in your eyes.

Check labels on materials before you use them. Look for the word *nontoxic,* which means "not poisonous."

Cover your skin if you have a cut or scratch. Some art materials, such as clay, can make cuts sting.

Show respect for other students. Walk carefully around their work. Never touch classmates' work without asking first.

Keep your area clean and neat. Clean up spills right away so no one will fall. Put materials back when you finish with them.

Tell your teacher if you have allergies or breathing problems. Some people are allergic to the kinds of dust in some art materials.

Always wash your hands after using art materials.

Trying Ways to Draw

There are lots of ways to draw. You can draw quickly to show action, or you can draw very carefully to show just how something looks to you. Try to draw every day. Keep your drawings in your sketchbook so that you can see how your work changes.

Here are some ideas for drawing. To start, get out your sketchbook or a sheet of paper and some pencils and markers.

SCRIBBLE DRAWING

Scribble drawing is a fun way to draw people. It helps you see the **proportions** of a person's body. Proportion is the size of one thing compared to another. For example, the upper and lower parts of an arm are about the same length.

Ask someone to pose for you. Have the person hold each pose for only about ten seconds. Use a marker to draw a scribble drawing of each pose. Work very quickly.

• **Scribble the head.**
  (Don't draw the neck.)
• **Scribble the body.**
• **Scribble the legs and the feet.**
• **Scribble the arms and the hands.**

CONTOUR DRAWING

Look closely at an object you want to draw. Start with the lines that go around shapes, which are called **contours**. Use your finger to trace around the contours of the objects in this picture.

To make a contour drawing, draw all the edges and shapes. Try making a contour drawing of this picture. Make your drawing much bigger than the picture. Look at the picture carefully as you draw. Find all the shapes, edges, and lines.

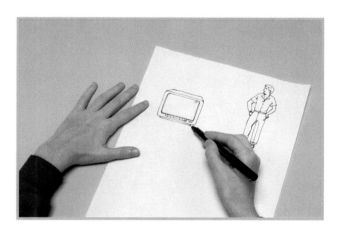

Now try making a contour drawing of a real object, such as a television set. You can even try a contour drawing of a person.

SHADING

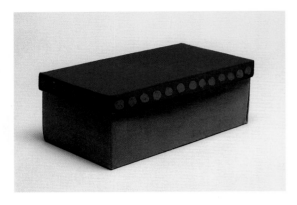

You can also show the shape of something without using contour lines at all. Look at the photograph of the box. Notice which areas are dark and which are light. Then look at the drawing of the box. It was made by using shading. Even without contour lines, you can tell what the object is.

Try other ways to show dark areas. Draw two small boxes. Fill one in with a pattern of dots, lines (hatching), or crosshatching. Fill the other with the same pattern drawn bigger. Which box looks darker?

The darkness or lightness of a color is its value. Experiment with your pencil. How many values can you make? Try smudging parts of your shading with a tissue. Then try erasing parts of your shading to make bright spots called **highlights**.

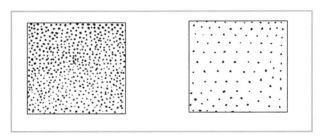

Now try drawing a simple object like a book without using lines. Look at the object closely. Notice that you may need to make some areas very dark and some areas lighter. Add highlights if you need to.

CONTOURS AND SHADING

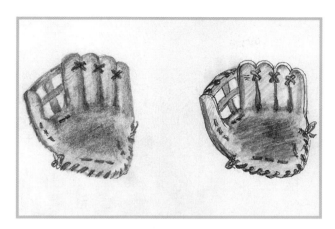

Try combining contour drawing with shading. Start by doing a drawing of something with an interesting shape, like a baseball mitt. Look at it carefully to see dark and light tones. Don't use any contour lines. Then look at the object again to see its contours. Add the outline, edges, and other contour lines.

You can also try this by starting with a contour drawing. Be sure you draw the outline of each shape and detail. Then add shading or patterns.

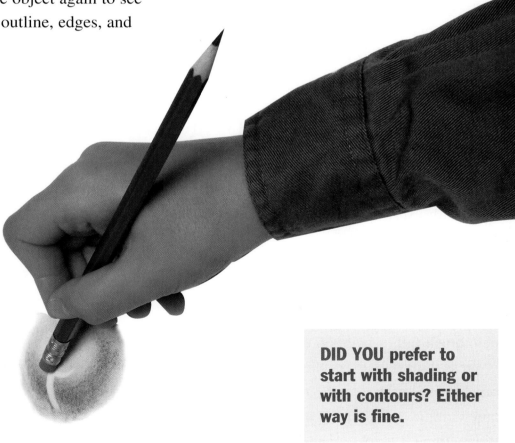

DID YOU prefer to start with shading or with contours? Either way is fine.

Experimenting with Paint

Painting is fun because you get to work with colors. Experimenting with paints will help you learn how artists use color and how to use color in your own artwork.

These are some things you should have when you paint: old newspapers to cover your work area, an old shirt to cover your clothes, tempera paints or watercolors, old dishes or plastic egg cartons for mixing paint, paper, paintbrushes, a jar or bowl of water, and paper towels.

TEMPERA PAINTS

Tempera paints are sometimes called poster paints. They are water-based, so they are easy to clean up. The colors are bright and easy to mix.

● GETTING STARTED

Start experimenting by dipping your paintbrush into one color. Try different kinds of brushstrokes—long and short, thin and light, wide and heavy.

Now clean your paintbrush and experiment with another color. Twist a paintbrush full of paint on the paper. Roll it, press it, or dab it. Try these different brushstrokes with lots of paint on the brush and with the brush almost dry. (You can dry it by wiping it across a paper towel.)

Get a fresh sheet of paper. Make a pattern or a picture, using some of these methods of painting. Try using a different color for each method.

MIXING COLORS

Even if you only have a few colors of tempera paints, you can mix them to make almost any color you want. An old saucer makes a good palette for mixing paint. You can also use a plastic egg carton.

Try making shades and tints. To make colors darker (shades), add black. Add white to make them lighter (tints). See how many shades and tints of a single color you can make.

TECHNIQUES TO TRY

Pour paint into a squeeze bottle (like the kind used for mustard). Stir a little liquid starch into the paint, and put the lid back on. Now hold the bottle over a piece of paper and squeeze gently to make lines and blobs. Use two or three colors to make a design or a picture. If you don't want the colors to mix, let each one dry before adding the next one.

Mix a little paint with the same amount of water. Drop a little blob of the thinned paint in the middle of your paper. Then blow at the paint through a straw to move it around. Drop blobs of other colors on the paper and blow them around. If you want the colors to mix, work quickly to blow them together.

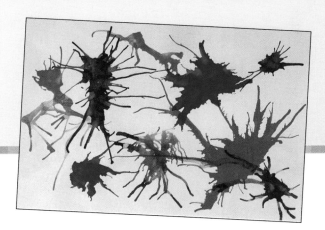

WATERCOLORS

Watercolors usually come in little dry cakes. You add the water! So keep a jar of clean water and some paper towels nearby as you paint. Paint on paper that is made for watercolors.

● GETTING STARTED

To start experimenting with watercolors, put a few drops of water on each cake of paint. Then dip your paintbrush in clean water and dab it in one of the colors. Try some different brushstrokes. Watercolors should be **transparent**; you should still see the paper beneath the paint. Use different amounts of water. What happens to the color when you use a lot of water?

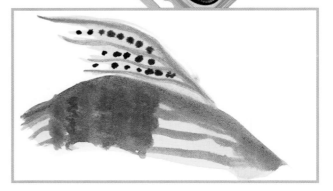

Now rinse your paintbrush in the water and try another color. Make lots of brushstrokes. Try thick lines and thin lines. Make squiggles, dots, and blobs. Change colors often, rinsing after each.

Try adding onto brushstrokes that are already dry. Work quickly to keep the colors clear. If your brushstrokes are too slow, the colors can get muddy. If you want part of your painting to be white, don't paint on it. The white comes from the color of the paper.

BE SURE TO CLEAN your paintbrushes and your work area when you have finished.

● MIXING COLORS

Experiment with mixing watercolors right on your paper. Try painting with a very wet paintbrush over a dry color. Try a wet color on or just touching another wet color. Try three colors together.

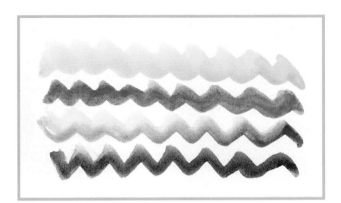

You can also mix colors on your paintbrush. Dip your paintbrush into one color and then another before you paint. Try this with blue and yellow. Clean your paintbrush and try some other combinations. To clean any paint cakes that you have used for mixing, wipe them with a paper towel.

TECHNIQUES TO TRY

Try making a wash. Start with a stripe of dark blue. Then clean your paintbrush and get it very wet. Use it to "wash" the color down the page. (You can use a wide paintbrush or a sponge for this.) Also try brushing clean water onto the paper. Then brush a stroke of color across it and let it spread by itself. Try two or three color washes together. For a special effect, sprinkle salt onto a wet wash.

Try a crayon-resist picture. Since watercolors don't cover crayons, you can make interesting designs and pictures by using both of them together. Draw a design or a picture with crayons. Leave lots of white paper. Then cover the paper with a light watercolor wash. Try it again with different colors.

Working with Clay

Clay is a special kind of earth that holds together and is easy to shape when it is mixed with water. Water-based clays can be fired—baked at a high temperature—or just left out in the air to dry until hard.

Start your work on a clean, dry surface. (A brown paper bag makes a good work surface.) Have some water handy to work into your clay if it starts to dry out. Use only a couple of drops at a time. When you are not working with it, store clay in a plastic bag to keep it from drying out.

Have some tools available. Use them to help you shape clay or to add texture or designs to things you make out of clay. You can use a rolling pin, toothpicks, a plastic fork and knife, a pencil, and other tools.

Start working with a piece of clay by making sure it has no air bubbles in it. Press it down, fold it over, and press it down again. This process is called **kneading**.

MODELING CLAY

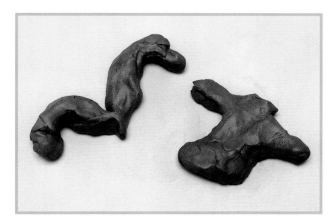

Try making different forms with your clay. One of your forms may remind you of an animal or a person. Model, or shape, forms by pinching and pulling the clay.

Try adding patterns, textures, or details to your form. Experiment with your tools. Press things into the clay and lift them off. Carve into the clay with a pencil. Try making patterns by combining the shapes you made with your tools. Press burlap into your clay and lift it off to add texture. If you change your mind, smooth the clay with your fingers and try something else.

To join shaped pieces, score, or carve lines in, each piece and wet them. Or you can coat the pieces with slip, which is clay mixed with water until it is like cream. Then press the pieces together and smooth the seams.

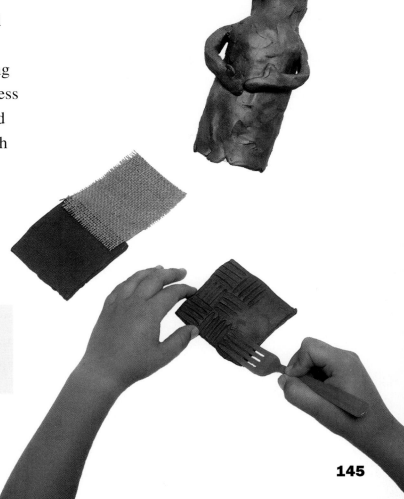

TO MAKE A BIGGER FORM, try modeling your clay around tubes or crumpled newspaper.

PINCHING

To make a pinch pot, start by molding a chunk of clay into a ball. Then press your thumb into the ball and pinch the clay against your fingers. Start at the bottom and work up, slowly pressing and smoothing the clay with your fingers. Keep turning the ball of clay as you work to make the sides an even thickness.

You can use pinch pots in sculpture. Two joined together can make the body of a figure. Leave a little hole in the bottom to allow air to escape if the figure is fired.

USING SLABS

Roll your clay out flat. It should be between a quarter of an inch and half an inch thick. If it is soft, you can shape it by draping it over something like a bowl or crumpled paper.

To make a slab box, roll your clay out flat. Cut two squares the same size with a plastic knife. One square will be the bottom of your box and the other will be the top. To make the sides, cut four rectangles the same length as the square. (Later you can try this with other shapes.) Let the pieces dry until they feel like leather. Join the pieces with slip. Then smooth the seams with your fingers.

USING COILS

To make a coil pot, roll pieces of clay against a hard surface to make long ropes. Use your whole hand, from your fingertips to your palms.

Make the bottom of your pot by coiling a rope of clay in a circle. Smooth the coil with your fingers.

To build your pot, place a rope of clay around the edge of the bottom. Keep adding ropes, and continue the coiling until your pot is as high as you want it. Smooth the inside as you work. You may smooth the outside or let the coils show.

YOU CAN also use clay coils to make figures.

147

Exploring Printmaking

When you make a print, you transfer color from one object to another. If you have ever left a hand-print on a window, you know what a print is. Here are some printmaking ideas to try.

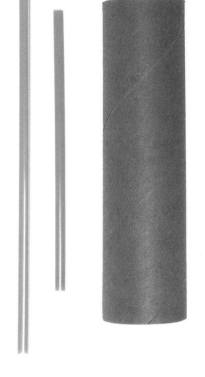

STAMP PRINTS

To make stamp prints, you will need tempera paints, paper in different colors, a flat tray such as an old cookie sheet, some paper towels or sponges, and some tools to print with. Try these to start: buttons, drinking straws, cotton swabs, small boxes, tubes of different sizes, pieces of cardboard.

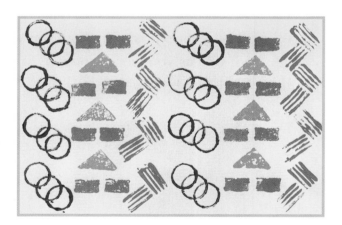

Start by putting damp paper towels or sponges on the cookie sheet. Spread a small amount of paint on each one. Keep the colors apart. Choose a piece of paper to print on. Press a tool into the paint, and then press it onto the paper. Try all your tools.

Now try using different colors and tools to make a pattern. Group shapes and repeat them. If you want to stamp one shape over another, let one dry first.

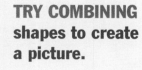

TRY COMBINING shapes to create a picture.

BLOCK PRINTING

Make a block print. You will need water-based printing ink or tempera paint, a flat pan, a brayer (a roller for printing) or a wide brush, a flat sheet of plastic foam cut from a meat tray, pieces of thin cardboard, and paper to print on.

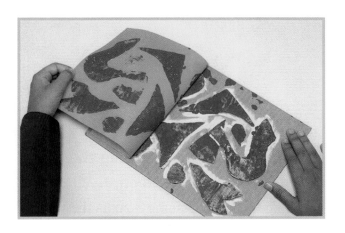

To make a printing block, draw a picture or design on the plastic foam. Be sure to press hard. Place the printing block on the newspaper. Roll or brush ink or paint over the picture. Then press a sheet of paper onto the block. Rub the paper gently, without letting it slide. Pull the paper off carefully. Let your print dry.

Here is another way to make a printing block. Cut shapes out of thin cardboard. Experiment with arranging the shapes until you like the design. Try overlapping some of them. Then glue them to a larger piece of cardboard to make a printing block. Cover the printing block with ink or paint. Press paper over it, and carefully rub the paper all over. Pull the paper off, and let it dry.

You can make several prints from the same printing block. Try printing on different colors of paper. Or rinse the printing block off and print with another color.

149

Displaying Your Artwork

Artists like to share their work by displaying it in museums or galleries. You can display your artwork and share it with your friends and family.

DISPLAYING PICTURES

A simple way to display several pictures is to hang them up.
Choose pictures that go together. Attach a strong string across a wall. Use clothespins or paper clips to hang your pictures.

Make a picture frame. Use a piece of cardboard that is longer and wider than your work. On the cardboard, draw a rectangle that is smaller than your picture. Have an adult cut out the rectangle. Decorate your frame with colors and patterns that look good with your picture.

Mount your picture by gluing the corners to a piece of cardboard. The cardboard should be the same size as the frame. Measure carefully to be sure your picture is centered. Then glue the frame to the cardboard. Tape thread on the back. Hang up your framed artwork.

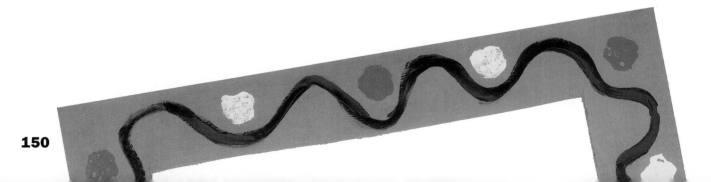

DISPLAYING SCULPTURES

Choose a safe place to display your sculptures. A table in a corner is a good place. Then choose a color of construction paper that looks good with your art. Cover an area a little larger than your work with the construction paper. If necessary, tape pieces of paper together and turn them over so that the tape doesn't show. You may want to cut the construction paper in an interesting shape.

Small sculptures that are not heavy can be displayed on stands. A stand holds the sculpture up so that it can be seen easily. Start with a small, sturdy box that is wider and longer than your sculpture. Turn it upside down. Choose a color that looks good with your art. Paint the sides, bottom and top of the box with tempera paint.

INVITE YOUR family and friends to see your art.

ELEMENTS & PRINCIPLES

Have you ever thought of art as a language?

Art communicates feelings, stories, and ideas. The **elements of art and principles of design** are like the words and sentences of the language of art. They are the tools artists use to communicate.

This section will show you the elements and principles. You may want to return to this section now and then to help you think about art.

As you learn more about the elements and principles, try to notice line, shape, and pattern all around you. Think about how artists, including yourself, use color, balance, and texture. Learn to look for and use the language of art.

Line

horizontal

straight

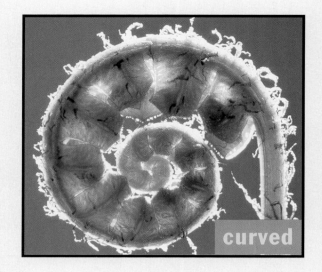

curved

diagonal

zigzag

vertical

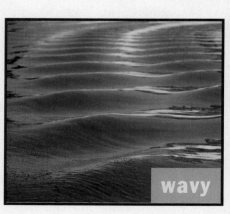

wavy

Texture

soft

rough

silky

smooth

bumpy

155

Shape

geometric

circle

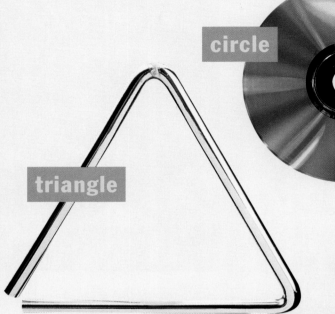

oval

triangle

rectangle

square

symbols and letters

organic

Form

geometric

sphere

pyramid

cone

cube

cylinder

organic

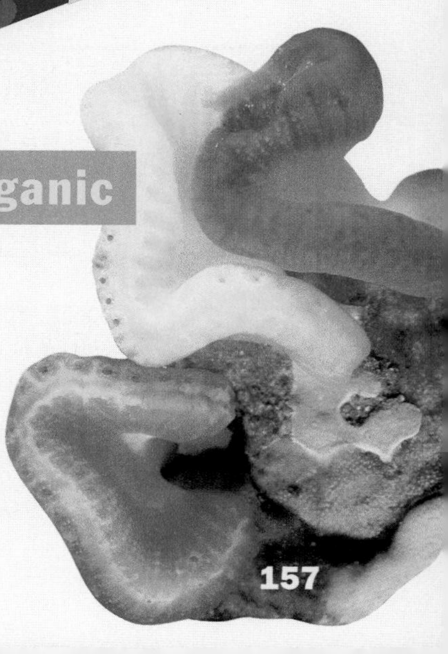

Color

complementary

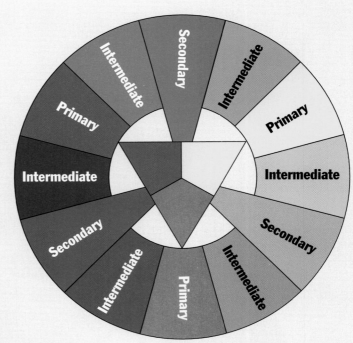

warm

cool

Value

shadows

light to dark

tint

shade

Space

positive, negative

proportion

background

middle ground

foreground

point of view

eye level

worm's eye

bird's eye

Unity

repeated lines,
textures, colors,
shapes, forms

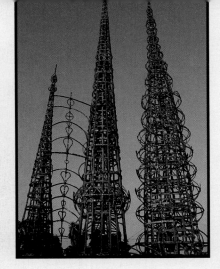

Variety

different lines, textures,
colors, shapes, forms

Movement and Rhythm

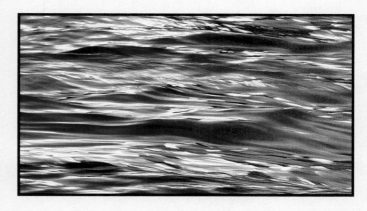

Proportion

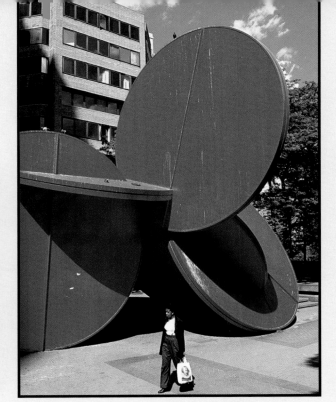

Balance

asymmetrical

symmetrical

physical balance

GALLERY OF ARTISTS

Judith Baca (1946–) United States, painter. Judith Baca [BAH•kah] was born in Los Angeles, California, and has spent her life working to bring people of all backgrounds together. She hopes that her community murals will help people from different cultures understand each other. **page 103**

Thomas Hart Benton (1889–1975) United States, painter. Thomas Hart Benton began his career as a newspaper cartoonist. He later became known for his pictures of rural America as well as biblical and historical subjects. Benton's murals can be found in many museums and public buildings in the United States. **page 18**

Albert Bierstadt (1830–1902) United States, painter. Born in Germany, Albert Bierstadt [BEER•stat] spent his childhood in Bedford, Massachusetts. After studying art in Germany and Italy as a young man, he returned to the United States. He is best known for his large and realistic landscapes. **page 32**

Gutzon Borglum (1867–1941) United States, sculptor. Gutzon Borglum was a successful painter before he became well-known as a sculptor. His best-known sculptures are the four U.S. presidents carved into the face of Mt. Rushmore. **page 38**

Margaret Bourke-White (1904–1971) United States, photographer. Margaret Bourke-White was one of America's best-known photojournalists. She was introduced to photography by her father. Her first subjects were factories and machines; she was interested in how they worked. She joined *Life* magazine when it began in 1936. She traveled around the world photographing historic sites and events. **pages 94, 96**

Alexander Calder
(1898–1976) United States, painter and sculptor. Alexander Calder was trained as an engineer. This influenced his work as a sculptor. He is best known for his mobiles. Calder's work also includes textile designs, jewelry, prints, and paintings. **pages 122-123, 129**

George Catlin
(1796–1872) United States, painter. George Catlin [KAT•luhn] taught himself how to paint portraits. Starting in 1832, he spent six years painting American Indians. He made nearly five hundred paintings of people and scenes from forty-eight different tribes. **page 41**

Paul Cézanne
(1839–1906) France, painter. When Paul Cézanne [say•ZAHN] looked at things in nature, he saw cylinders, spheres, cones, and other geometric forms. His works were not understood or liked by people of his time. But his ideas led to an art movement called Cubism. Today he is considered a great artist. **pages 22, 23**

Lynne Cherry (1952–) United States, illustrator. As a child, Lynne Cherry loved to draw scenes from nature. Her book illustrations, which promote protection of wildlife, have earned her many awards. **pages 12, 66**

Allan Rohan Crite
(1910–) United States, painter. Allan Crite is best known for his paintings of city neighborhoods in the 1930s and 1940s. Many show children and reflect the fashions and architecture of the times. **page 52**

Salvador Dalí
(1904–1989) Spain, painter. Salvador Dalí [dah•LEE] was one of the most famous Surrealist artists. Dalí called his paintings "dream photographs." Talented in many fields, Dalí also designed jewelry, advertisements, costumes, and stage settings. **page 116**

Edgar Degas
(1834–1917) France, painter. Edgar Degas [duh•GAH] was fascinated by photographic techniques. In many of his paintings, Degas captured his subjects in a revealing moment, as if on film. Degas painted many pictures of dancers, often in rehearsal or backstage. **page 49**

Maurits Cornelis Escher
(1898–1972) Holland, graphic artist. Maurits Cornelis Escher [EH•sher] studied architecture, but became a graphic artist instead. He is famous for drawings that surprise viewers with optical illusions. **page 130**

Janet Fish (1938–) United States, painter. Janet Fish grew up knowing she wanted to be an artist like her mother and grandfather. Her realistic paintings show light reflected through glass, water, and mirrors. She says, "My real subject is the movement of light and color from one form to another." Because changes in weather change the way colors look, she always works on two paintings at the same time—one for cloudy days and one for sunny days. **page 14**

Paul Gauguin
(1848–1903) France, painter. Paul Gauguin [goh•GAN] grew up in France. He was a sailor in the French navy and a stockbroker before deciding to devote his life to painting at the age of 35. In 1895 Gauguin moved to the tropical island of Tahiti. He lived and painted in the tropics for the rest of his life. **page 31**

Barbara Hepworth
(1903–1975) England, sculptor. Barbara Hepworth said that the hilly English countryside influenced the shapes in her work. Most of her sculptures have a curved shape and are pierced with holes to give an airy feeling. **page 125**

David Hockney (1937–) England, mixed media. British-born artist David Hockney lives in southern California. He was only 11 years old when he decided he wanted to be an artist. Hockney has said, "The smallest event can become a story if you tell it in the right way." **page 118**

Katsushika Hokusai
(1760–1849)
Japan, printmaker.
Katsushika Hokusai
[kaht•soo•SHEE•kah
HOH•koo•sy] learned the art of wood block engraving at the age of fourteen. His ability to capture nature's awesome power made him the greatest artist from a school of Japanese printmakers. He produced about 30,000 pictures in his lifetime. **page 25**

Winslow Homer
(1836–1910) United States, painter and illustrator. Winslow Homer was fascinated by the ocean and painted many works that show the coasts of Maine (where he lived), the Bahamas, Cuba, and Florida. Humans struggling against the powerful sea is another theme in his paintings. **page 50**

Luis Jiménez (1940–)
United States, sculptor. Mexican American artist Luis Jiménez [hee•MAY•nes] began his art career working in his father's neon sign shop. His art celebrates working people and Latino culture in the United States. Many of his sculptures are built of fiberglass, shaped around metal frames, and painted with a glossy finish. **pages 54, 57**

Sargent Johnson
(1887–1967) United States, sculptor. Sargent Johnson's work first became popular in the 1930s. His goal was to celebrate and reflect on the lives and accomplishments of African Americans. His work was influenced by traditional African art and American jazz. **page 76**

Rockwell Kent
(1882–1971) United States, painter. Rockwell Kent based many of his paintings and illustrations on his journeys to Alaska, Greenland, and South America. He is the author of several travel-adventure books and an autobiography. **page 28**

Jacob Lawrence (1917–) United States, painter. Jacob Lawrence grew up in the Harlem neighborhood of New York City. His vivid story paintings show the history of African Americans. Cubist painters influenced his style. He chose this style because the simple, bold forms make his subjects seem like the heroes of legends. **page 50**

Roy Lichtenstein (1923–1997) United States, painter, sculptor. Roy Lichtenstein [LIK•tuhn•styn] is one of the best-known American painters in the Pop Art movement. His most famous paintings imitate comic strips. Lichtenstein paints the patterns of dots that newspapers use to print colors, and he often includes speech bubbles in his works. **pages 51, 72**

Tom Lochray (1959–) United States, graphic artist. Tom Lochray [LAHK•ray] lives in Minneapolis. His work is influenced by poster artists of the 1920s and 1930s and many contemporary artists. Lochray uses a computer to complete his artworks. Each one takes one to two weeks to complete. **page 70**

Jim Love (1927–) United States, sculptor. While studying business administration in college, Jim Love was introduced to art when he was asked to create theater sets. He later worked at the Contemporary Arts Museum in Houston. Love's sculptures are created from steel and bronze. Many of the metal pieces used in the sculptures were found in junk piles. **page 132**

René Magritte (1898–1967) Belgium, painter. René Magritte [muh•GREET] once worked as a wallpaper designer. Many of his paintings include repeated patterns like those used on wallpaper. Magritte usually painted dreamlike scenes. In them we see that there is more than one way of viewing the world. **page 117**

Marisol (1930–) United States, sculptor. Born in Venezuela, Marisol [mah•REE•sohl] shows her humorous but thoughtful views on modern life in her work. She carves life-size sculptures out of huge blocks of wood, and uses plaster casts of her own hands in some of them. Her sculptures show both ordinary and famous people. **page 128**

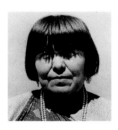

María Martínez (1887–1980) United States, potter and sculptor. For generations, making pottery has been an important part of María Martínez's family traditions. Many of her pots are black on black and highly polished, similar to ancient samples unearthed in the American Southwest. **page 74**

Claude Monet (1840–1926) France, painter. Claude Monet [moh•NAY] and his fellow French Impressionist painters became known for painting with small patches of color. From a distance, the patches of color blended together. Though never well-received by the art world in his day, Monet is considered a master artist today. **pages 19, 70**

Jesús Bautista Moroles (1950–) United States, sculptor. Jesús Bautista Moroles [hay•SOOS bow•TEES•tah moh•ROH•les] learned masonry, or the craft of cutting stone, from his uncle. He chooses interesting pieces of granite from stone quarries. He works on about twenty pieces at a time. To show the different qualities of the granite, he often leaves parts of the sculpture rough, and polishes other parts. **pages 98, 124**

Georgia O'Keeffe (1887–1986) United States, painter. Georgia O'Keeffe grew up on a farm in Wisconsin. She knew she wanted to be an artist by the age of thirteen. O'Keeffe became one of the most important American artists of the early twentieth century. Many of her most famous paintings show close-up views of flowers. Art critics have praised the bold shapes and intense colors of her paintings. **pages 24, 69**

José Clemente Orozco (1883–1949) Mexico, painter. José Clemente Orozco [hoh•SAY klay•MAYN•tay oh•ROHS•koh] lost his left hand in an accident when he was 17, but went on to become one of Mexico's most famous artists. Many of his works show scenes from the Mexican Revolution of the early 1900s. **page 48**

Frances "Fanny" Palmer (1812–1876) United States, printmaker. Frances Palmer made prints for Currier and Ives, a famous company that sold prints across the United States. She was the only highly successful woman in her field at the time. Her nineteenth-century scenes are still reproduced today on greeting cards and in advertisements. **page 71**

Becky Crouch Patterson (1945–) United States, textile artist. Becky Crouch Patterson creates scenes by sewing together various kinds of fabric. Landscapes, animals, and biblical stories inspire her artwork. **page 92**

Pablo Picasso (1881–1973) Spain, painter. Pablo Picasso was one of the great figures of the twentieth-century art world. His works changed the way people thought about art. Picasso helped found a movement in painting called Cubism. Cubist paintings use basic geometric shapes to show form. Picasso was heavily influenced by the style of African sculpture when he began painting in this style. **pages 34, 42, 44**

Jackson Pollock (1912–1956) United States, painter. Jackson Pollock [PAH•luhk] had a great influence on twentieth-century art. His paintings express powerful moods without using images. Although Pollock's designs may appear to be unplanned, he creates a sense of movement to produce an exciting composition. **page 119**

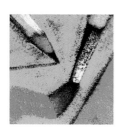

Martin Puryear (1941–) United States, sculptor. Martin Puryear grew up in Washington, D.C., near the Smithsonian museums. As a child, he spent much time in the museums, sketching the exhibits. He learned woodworking from his father and from craftsmen in Africa. Puryear often works in series when creating his sculptures. **page 114**

Frederic Remington (1861–1909) United States, sculptor and painter. The works of Frederic Remington are based on themes and subjects of the American frontier West. Although born in New York state, Remington spent a good deal of time in the West, documenting the lives of soldiers and cowboys. **page 56**

Rembrandt van Rijn (1606–1669) Holland, painter. Rembrandt van Rijn (known as Rembrandt) is considered one of Europe's greatest artists. Over the course of his life he created nearly 600 paintings, 300 etchings, and 1,400 drawings. His subjects included portraits, landscapes, and biblical and historical scenes. He is known for his sympathetic and powerful portraits of people. **page 36**

Diego Rivera (1886–1957) Mexico, muralist. Diego Rivera is famous for his monumental murals. Most are located in Mexico City, but quite a few can be seen in the United States, along with many of his smaller paintings and drawings. Rivera was only ten years old when he began taking art courses in Mexico City. He has said, "In my work, I tell the story of my nation, Mexico— its history, its Revolution, its amazing Indian past, and its present-day popular traditions." **page 45**

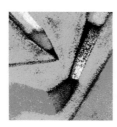

Rachel Ruysch (1664–1750) Holland, painter. Rachel Ruysch [RYSH] was the daughter of a Dutch botany professor. She used her knowledge of plants in her still lifes of flowers. She began her formal study of painting when she was only fifteen, and was still painting in her eighties. Ruysch liked to hide snakes, lizards, and insects among the flowers and fruit in her still lifes. **page 30**

Augustus Saint-Gaudens (1848–1907) United States, sculptor. Augustus Saint-Gaudens [saynt•GAWD•uhnz] was born in Ireland but grew up in New York City. He first learned sculpture by working as a cameo maker, carving relief portraits for jewelry. Saint-Gaudens's bronze statues and relief sculptures are prized for their expressiveness. **pages 39, 99**

Charles M. Schulz (1922–) United States, cartoonist. Charles M. Schulz [SHULTS] was born in Minnesota. His cartoons were rejected by his high school yearbook, but he did not give up. Eventually, newspapers began printing his comic strips. Schulz created his famous *Peanuts* characters in 1950. He based the comic's hero, Charlie Brown, on himself as a child. *Peanuts* is printed in over 2,000 newspapers in 70 countries around the world. **page 58**

Georges Seurat (1859–1891) France, painter. Known as the founder of Neo-Impressionism, Georges Seurat [soo•RAH] painted huge compositions that seem to shimmer. His technique of showing light by using tiny brushstrokes of contrasting colors is called Pointillism. **page 126**

Charles Sheeler (1883–1965) United States, painter and photographer. Charles Sheeler was known as a Precisionist because of the precise way in which he painted the skyscrapers, factories, and barns of the American landscape. His painting style was influenced by photography and by Cubist painters, who represented form with simple geometric shapes. **page 68**

John Steptoe (1950–1989) United States, illustrator. John Steptoe wrote his first book at the age of sixteen, while attending the High School of Art and Design in New York City. Through his award-winning illustrations, Steptoe hoped to inspire young people to achieve their dreams. **page 46**

Margaret Tafoya

(1904–) United States, potter. Margaret Tafoya learned to make pottery from her mother while growing up in Santa Clara Pueblo, New Mexico. Along with traditional pottery methods, Tafoya has developed her own version of the Pueblo style. Tafoya has taught her children and grandchildren to make pottery. **page 82**

Vincent van Gogh

(1835–1890) Holland, painter. Vincent van Gogh [van GOH] sold only one painting when he was alive, but today he is recognized as one of the most famous painters in the world. He used bright colors and thick oil paint, making his brushstrokes easy to see. Van Gogh's paintings reveal his strong feelings about the beauty of nature. **page 68**

Diego Velázquez

(1599–1660) Spain, painter. Diego Velázquez [bay•LAHS•kes] was the court painter for King Philip IV of Spain. One of the artist's favorite techniques was to focus intense light on his subjects and set them against dark backgrounds. **pages 41, 43**

Andy Warhol

(1928?–1987) United States, painter. Andy Warhol was one of the most important artists in the Pop Art movement. In many of his works of art, Warhol used familiar commercial images but played with their colors and sizes, often repeating the images. **pages 64, 65**

GLOSSARY

The Glossary contains important art terms and their definitions. Each word is respelled as it would be in a dictionary. When you see this mark ´ after a syllable, pronounce that syllable with more force than the other syllables.

add, **ā**ce, **câ**re, **pä**lm; **e**nd, **ē**qual; **i**t, **ī**ce; **o**dd, **ō**pen, **ô**rder; t**ŏŏ**k, p**ōō**l; **u**p, b**û**rn; y**ōō** as *u* in *fuse*; **oi**l; p**ou**t; ə as *a* in *above*, *e* in *sicken*, *i* in *possible*, *o* in *melon*, *u* in *circus*; **ch**eck; ri**ng**; **th**in; **th**is; **zh** as in *vision*

abstract [ab´strakt] A style of art in which the artist uses unusual lines, colors, and shapes to make the subject look unrealistic. It is often characterized by the use of geometric lines and shapes and bold, bright colors.

abstract

action lines [ak´shən līnz] Lines used to create a sense of movement.

actual lines [ak´chə•wəl līnz] Lines that can be seen. (*See* implied lines.)

architecture [är´kə•tek•chər] The art of designing buildings.

asymmetrical balance [ā•sə•me´tri•kəl ba´ləns] The look of a design in which things on each side of a center line are unbalanced. (*See also* balance; symmetrical balance.)

background [bak´ground] The part of an artwork that appears farthest in the distance.

balance [ba´ləns] The arrangement of elements in a work of art. There are three kinds of balance: symmetrical balance, asymmetrical balance, and radial balance. (*See also* asymmetrical balance, radial balance, symmetrical balance.)

bird's-eye view [bûrd´zī vyo͞o] A point of view looking down from above. (*See also* worm's-eye view.)

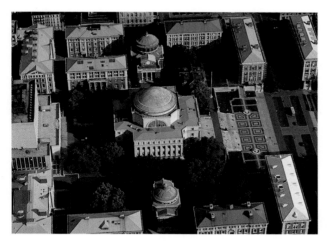

bird's eye view

cartoonist [kär•to͞o´nist] An artist who creates the words and pictures in cartoons and comic strips.

cathedral [kə•thē´drəl] Any large or important church.

cathedral

cave paintings [kāv pān´tingz] Pictures painted on cave walls that tell stories about life nearly 40,000 years ago.

center of interest [sen´tər əv in´trest] The part of an artwork that stands out.

ceremonial [ser•ə•mō´nē•əl] Traditions or items used in a formal or strict way.

cityscape [si´tē•skāp] A painting or drawing showing a whole or partial view of a city.

cityscape

coat of arms [kōt əv ärmz] A design used as the symbol of a family, an organization, or a nation.

coat of arms

collage [kə•läzh´] A work of art created by gluing bits of paper, fabric, scraps, photographs, or other materials to a flat surface.

color [kəl´ər] The hue, value, and intensity of an object.

comic strips [kä´mik strips] Several pictures with words that have been put together to tell a story.

continuous line [kən•tin´yōō•əs līn] A line not having a beginning or an end that can be seen.

continuous line

contour line [kon´tōōr līn] The outer edge of an object.

contrast [kon´trast] The difference between the colors or shapes of two things that makes one or both stand out.

cool colors [kōōl kəl´ərz] The family of colors that goes from greens through blues to violets. (*See also* warm colors.)

curved line [kûrvd līn] A rounded line.

depth [depth] The apparent distance from front to back or near to far in an artwork.

detail [dē´tāl] A part of an object or a scene that can be seen most clearly close up.

diagonal line [dī•a´gə•nəl līn] A line that slants.

diorama [dī•ə•ra´mə] A scene, usually smaller than in real life, in which three-dimensional models are displayed against a realistic painted background.

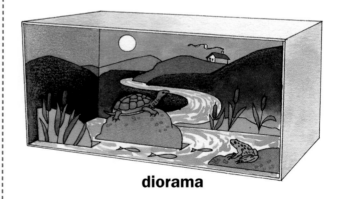

diorama

emphasis [em´fə•sis] Drawing attention to certain areas or objects in a work of art by using different sizes, shapes, and lines; contrasting colors; and intense, bright colors.

foreground [fôr´ground] The part of an artwork that looks closest to the viewer.

foreground

form [fôrm] The three-dimensional shape of an object. Forms have many sides.

geometric [jē•ə•me´trik] Based on simple shapes such as rectangles, triangles, circles, or straight lines.

illusion [i•lo͞o´zhən] Created to trick the eye.

implied lines [im•plīd´ līnz] Hidden lines. (*See also* actual lines.)

Impressionism [im•pre´shə•ni•zəm] An art movement that concentrated on showing the effects of light on things at different times of day. Impressionists used unblended dots and slashes of pure color placed close together to create a mood or an impression of a scene.

kiln [kiln] A very hot oven used to harden clay.

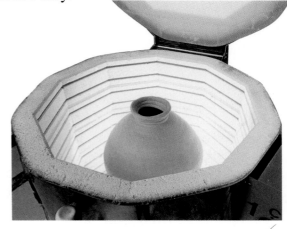

kiln

landscape [land´skāp] A scene showing a large area of land that may include mountains, rivers, flowers, fields, or forests.

lead [led] A kind of soft metal often used in stained glass to hold together the pieces of colored glass.

line [līn] The connection between two or more points.

maquette [ma•ket´] A scale model used to plan a full-sized object.

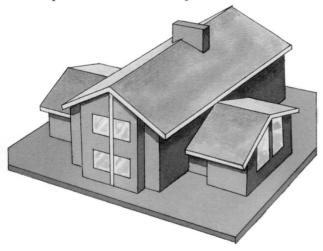

maquette

marionette [mar•ē•ə•net´] A wooden puppet that is moved by pulling strings attached to different parts of its body.

marionette

mask [mask] An artwork worn over the face.

memorial [mə•môr´ē•əl] A statue or another structure created to remind us of people or events.

middle ground [mi´dəl ground] The part of an artwork that lies between the foreground and the background.

mobile [mō´bēl] A type of sculpture in which objects are suspended and balanced so that they are moved by currents of air.

mobile

monochromatic [mo•nə•krō•ma´tik] Of or having one color.

mood [mood] A feeling or an emotion.

mosque [mosk] A place of public worship for Muslims.

mosque

movement [moov´mənt] A sense of motion.

mural [myoor´əl] A very large painting that covers a wall. It can be painted right on the wall or painted on paper, canvas, or wood that is attached to the wall.

negative shapes [ne´gə•tiv shāps] The shapes around a positive shape or form. (*See also* positive shapes.)

nonrepresentational art [non•re•pri•zen•tā´shə•nəl ärt] Art that does not look like anything that is known.

organic shapes [ôr•ga´nik shāps] Rounded, uneven shapes like those found in nature.

origami [ôr•ə•gä´mē] The art of folding paper.

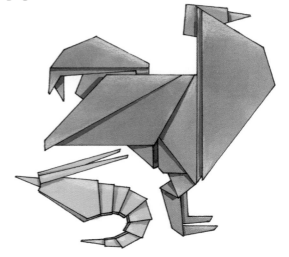

origami

ornaments [ôr´nə•mənts] Decorations added to objects.

outline [out´līn] The line that forms the shape of something.

overlapping [ō•vər•lap´ing] A technique in which one shape or part covers up some or all of another.

papier-mâché [pā•pər•mə•shā´] An art material made of paper torn into strips or made into pulp and mixed with art paste.

pattern [pa´tərn] Repeating shapes, lines, or colors in a design.

petroglyphs [pe´trə•glifs] Carvings on rocks.

photographer [fə•tä´grə•fər] A person who uses a camera to take photographs.

photography [fə•tä´grə•fē] The art of taking pictures with a camera.

point of view [point əv vyo͞o] The view of something from a certain place.

portrait [pôr´trət] A painting, sculpture, drawing, photo, or other work of art showing a person, several people, or an animal.

positive shapes [pä´zə•tiv shāps] The shapes in a work of art. (*See also* negative shapes.)

potter [pä´tər] A person who makes objects from clay.

pottery [pä´tə•rē] Objects made from clay.

pottery

primary colors [prī´mer•ē kəl´ərz] The colors red, yellow, and blue. The primary colors are mixed together to form other colors. (*See also* secondary colors.)

print [print] A picture created by using a stamp or stencil.

profile [prō´fīl] The side view of a person or an object.

profile

proportion [prə•pôr´shən] The size of one thing compared to the size of another.

puppet [pu´pət] A toy usually made from wood or cloth that can be used to act out a story or play.

pyramid [pir´ə•mid] A form that has a flat base and three or more sides shaped like triangles. These triangles slope upward to meet in a point at the top.

radial balance [rā´de•əl ba´ləns] Shown in circular designs that are arranged evenly around a center. (*See also* balance.)

radial balance

realistic [rē•ə•lis´tik] Something that looks real.

relief sculpture [ri•lēf´ skulp´chər] Images carved onto a surface so that they stand out from the background.

repetition [re•pə•ti´shən] Something that repeats itself.

rhythm [ri´thəm] The regular repetition of lines, shapes, colors, or patterns in a work of art.

scale [skāl] The ratio of the size of parts in a drawing or another artwork to their size in the original. If a picture is drawn to scale, all of its parts are equally smaller or larger than the original.

sculpture [skulp´chər] A carving, model, or other three-dimensional piece of art.

secondary colors [se´kən•der•ē kəl´ərz] The colors orange, green, and violet. They are created by combining two of the three primary colors. (*See also* primary colors.)

shade [shād] A color to which black has been added to make that color darker. (*See also* tint.)

shadow puppet [sha´dō pu´pət] A type of puppet that is held up behind a thin screen. When light shines on the puppet from behind the screen, the puppet casts a shadow.

shadow puppet

shape [shāp] A two-dimensional figure outlined by lines or a change in color or shading. (See also geometric, organic shapes.)

space [spās] The distance, area, or depth shown in a work of art. Also the open parts between or inside shapes.

stained glass [stānd glas] An art form in which colored glass pieces are cut and arranged in beautiful designs. The designs are held together with lead.

stained glass

still life [stil līf] An arrangement of mostly nonliving objects shown in a work of art.

style [stīl] The way an artist chooses to show a subject.

stylized [stī′ə•līzd] Type of art in which details are left out and objects are shown as simple shapes.

Surrealist [sə•rē′ə•list] A style of painting that shows dreamlike images. Surrealistic artists put together unusual or impossible combinations of things and paint them in a realistic way.

symbols [sim′bəlz] Lines, shapes, or colors that stand for things or ideas.

symmetrical balance [sə•me′tri•kəl ba′ləns] The look of a design in which things on each side of a center line are balanced. (*See also* asymmetrical balance, balance.)

texture [teks′chər] The way a surface looks and feels, such as rough or smooth.

three-dimensional [thrē•də•men′shə•nəl] Having length, width, and depth. A sculpture is three-dimensional, but a drawing is two-dimensional because it does not have depth. (*See also* two-dimensional.)

two-dimensional

three-dimensional

tint [tint] A color to which white has been added to make that color lighter. (*See also* shade.)

translucent [trans•lōō•sənt] Something through which light can be seen.

two-dimensional [tōō•də•men´shə•nəl] Having height and width, but not depth; flat. (*See also* three-dimensional.)

unity [yōō´nə•tē] The balance and organization of the elements in an artwork to create a pleasing design.

value [val´yōō] The lightness or darkness of a color.

variety [və•rī´ə•tē] An assortment of lines, colors, forms, shapes, or textures in a work of art.

vessels [ves´əlz] Containers for holding liquids.

warm colors [wärm kəl´ərz] The family of colors that goes from reds through oranges to yellows. (*See also* cool colors.)

watercolor [wô´tər•kəl´ər] A kind of paint made by mixing powdered colors with a binding agent and water. The term also refers to a painting done with watercolors.

worm's-eye view [wûrm´zī vyōō] A point of view from ground level. (*See also* bird's-eye view.)

worm's-eye view

ARTISTS & ARTWORKS

INDEX

A

Abstract, 42–43
Activities
See Production activities.
Architecture, 88–89, 108–109
Art and Culture
Formal Portraits, 40–41
Origami, 80–81
Art and Literature
John Steptoe Paints a Story, 46–47
Lynne Cherry's World, 66–67
Say It with Pictures, 100–101
Artists
See Gallery of Artists, 166–175; Index of Artists and Artworks, 186–187.
Artworks
See Gallery of Artists, 166–175; Index of Artists and Artworks, 186–187.
Asymmetrical balance, 105, 165

B

Background, 19, 159
Balance
asymmetrical, 105, 165
in a mobile, 122–123
radial, 84–85, 110–111
symmetrical, 105, 165
Bird's-eye view, 96, 159
Block printing, 149

C

Careers in Art
Animator, 60–61
Park Designer, 106–107
Cartoonist, 58–59
Cathedral, 108
Cave painting, 16–17
Celebration Art
Fireworks, 86–87

Center of interest

Center of interest, 30–31
Cityscape, 68–69
Clay, 39, 57, 83, 144–147
See also Production activities.
Coat of arms, 62–63
Collage, 105
Color
contrast, 25
monochromatic, 45
primary, 43, 158
secondary, 43, 158
shades and tints, 45, 141
value, 24–25, 138, 141, 158
warm/cool, 44–45, 158
Comic strips, 58–59
Community Art
Topiary Garden, 126–127
Visiting a Museum, 20–21
Contour drawing, 137, 139

D

Diorama, 29
Displaying artwork, 150–151
Drawing, 17, 19, 25, 37, 43, 49, 51, 59, 109, 131, 136–139
See also Production activities.

E

Elements of art
color, 24, 44–45, 141, 158
form, 56, 124, 157
line, 17, 51, 59, 79, 154
shape, 17, 24, 37, 42, 69, 78, 99, 125, 156
space, 19, 28, 30, 159
texture, 39, 77, 145, 155
value, 24–25, 138, 141, 158
Elements and Principles, 152–165
See also Elements of art, Principles of design.
Emphasis, 25, 31, 161
Everyday Art
Auto Art, 120–121
Seeing Designs in Nature, 26–27

ACKNOWLEDGMENTS

PHOTO CREDITS:

Page Placement Key: (t)-top (c)-center (b)-bottom (l)-left (r)-right (fg)- foreground (bg)- background).

Cover: Christie's, London/Superstock, ©1997 Artists Rights Society (ARS), N.Y./ADAGP, Paris.

Frontmatter:

Harcourt Brace & Company:

Page 5 (t) Harcourt Brace & Co., 10-11, Richard Nowitz; 13 (All) Ron Kunzman.

Other:

4, Courtesy of Stewart & Stewart; 5 (b) Pete Saloutos/The Stock Market; 6 (l) Cummer Museum of Art and Gardens/Superstock; 6(r) & 7 (l), David T. Vernon/Colter Bay Indian Arts Museum, NPS; 7 (r) By Permission of Florence Temko, author of "Paper Pandas and Jumping Frogs," published by China Books, San Francisco; 8 Adam Woolfit/Woodfin Camp & Associates; 9 Gimpel Fils Gallery; 12 (t) Harcourt Brace & Company Children's Books; 12 (bl) Courtesy, Lynne Cherry; 12 (br) Illustration from The Great Kapok Tree: A Tale of the Amazon Rain Forest ©1990 by Lynne Cherry, reproduced by permission of Harcourt Brace & Company .

Unit 01:

Harcourt Brace & Company:

17 (b), 23 (b) 29 (b) 31 (b) & 33 Weronica Ankarorn.

Other:

14 Private Collection, Courtesy of the artist and D C Moore Gallery, New York. 15 (b) Courtesy of Stewart & Stewart; 16 (t) Curtis Schaafsma/Polly Schaafsma; 16 (b) Jean-Marie Chauvet/Sygma; 17 (t) Curtis Schaafsma/Polly Schaafsma; 18 ©1998 Thomas H. Benton & Rita P. Benton Testamentary Trusts/Licensed by VAGA, New York, NY; 19 (t)Christie's Images/Superstock; 19(b) Courtauld Institute & Galleries, London/Superstock; 20 Courtesy, San Antonio Museum of Art; 21 Brooke Savage, Courtesy, San Antonio Museum of Art; 22 (c)1992 The Barnes Foundation, all rights reserved; 23 (t) Museum of Modern Western Art, Moscow, Russia/Superstock; 24 Columbus Museum of Art, Ohio; Museum Purchase: Howald Fund II ©1998 The Georgia O'Keefe Foundation/Artists Rights Society (ARS), New York; 25 Art Resource, NY; 26 (l) & 26 (b)Cowan/West Stock; 27 (l) & 27 (t) Jerome Wexler; 28 Gift of Gertrude V. Whitney, #1923.51/The Art Institute of Chicago; 29 (t) Giraudon/Art Resource,NY; 30 Bridgeman/Art Resource, NY; 31 (t) The Museum of Modern Art, New York, Mrs. Simon Guggenheim Fund. Photograph 1998 The Museum of Modern Art, New York; 32-33 SuperStock.

Unit 02:

Harcourt Brace & Company:

39 (c) Harcourt Brace & Company; 37(b), 39 (b) Weronica Ankarorn; 40 (b) Ron Kunzman; 43 (b), 45 (b), & 51 (b), 53 Weronica Ankarorn.

Other:

34 Giraudon/Art Resource,NY ©1998 Estate of Pablo Picaso/Artists Rights Society (ARS), New York; 35 Herbert List/Magnum Photos; 36 The Norton Simon Foundaton, Pasadena, CA; 37 (t) Archives Division, Texas State Library; 38 Pete Saloutos/The Stock Market; 39 (t) National Museum Of American Art, Smithsonian Institution Gift of Rose Pitman Huges, Washington, D.C./Art Resource, NY; 40 (t) Brown Brothers; 41 (t) Scala/Art Resource, NY; 41 (b) National Gallery of Art,Washington, D.C./Superstock; 42 Museu Picasso, Barcelona, ©1998 Estate of Pablo Picaso/Artists Rights Society (ARS), New York; 43 (t) Museo de Prado, Madrid, Spain/Erich Lessing/Art Resource NY; 44 National Gallery Of Art, Washington. Chester Dale Collection, D. 1966 Board Of Trustees, ©1998 Estate of Pablo Picaso/Artists Rights Society (ARS), New York; 45(t) Education Secretariat, Mexico/E.T. Archive, London/Superstock; 46 & 47 Copyright (c) 1987 by John Steptoe. By permission of Lothrop, Lee & Shepard Books, a division of William Morrow & Company, Inc. with the approval of the John Steptoe Literary Trust; 48 The Museum of Modern Art, New York, given anonymously, Photograph ©1998 The Museum of Modern Art, New York.; 49 (t) A&F Pears Ltd., London/SuperStock; 49 (b) Anna Belle Lee Washington/Superstock; 50 (t) Courtesy of the artists and Francine Seders Gallery, Seattle, WA, photo by Spike Mafford; 50 (b) The Metropolitan Museum of Art, Gift of Christian A. Zabriskie, 1950. ©1992; 51 (t) Scottish National Gallery of Modern Art; 52 National Museum of American Art, Washington, D. C./Art Resource, NY.

Unit 03:

Harcourt Brace & Company:

57 (r) Don Couch; 59 Weronica Ankarorn; 63 (t) Harcourt Brace & Co./David

Toerge/Black Star; 63 (b), 65 (b) 69 (b) 71(b) & 73 Weronica Ankarorn; 70 (t) Art by Tom Lochray, Harcourt Brace & Company.

Other:

54 (l) Bruce Berman Photography; 54 (r) Courtesy, Luis Jimenez; 55 Bruce Berman Photography; 56 Cummer Museum of Art and Gardens/Superstock; 57(l) Werner Forman Archive/Art Resource; 58 PEANUTS reprinted by permission of United Feature Syndicate, Inc.; 60 (l) Gary Moss/Outline Press; 60 (r) & 61 Photofest; 62 (b) United States Department of State; 63 (tl) Texas State Secretary of State; 64 & 65 (t) ©1997 Andy Warhol Foundation for the Visual Arts/Artists Rights Society (ARS), NY/photo Art Resource, NY; 66 Harcourt Brace & Company Children's Books; 67 Illustration from The Armadillo from Amarillo, ©1994 by Lynne Cherry, reproduced by permission of Harcourt Brace & Company; 68 (l) Planet Art; 68 (r) Collection, Hirschl & Adler Galleries, New York; 69 (t) ©1997 The Georgia O'Keffe Foundation/Artists Rights Society(ARS), New York, photo by Malcolm Varon, NYC 1987; 70 (b) Planet Art; 71(b) Museum of City of New York/Superstock; 72 © Roy Lichtenstein.

Unit 04:

Harcourt Brace & Company:

77(b), 79 (b), 83 (b), 85 (b), 89 (b) 91 (b) & 93 Weronica Ankarorn.

Other:

74 The Museum of Fine Arts, Houston,Gift of Miss Ima Hogg; 75 U.S. Department of the Interior Indian Arts and Crafts Board; 76 San Francisco Museum Of Modern Art, Albert M. Bender Collection, Gift of Albert M. Bender., Photo, Ben Blackwell; 7(t), 78, 79 (t) From the Girard Foundation Collection in the Museum of International Folk Art, a unit of the Museum of New Mexico.; 80 By permission of Florence Temko, author of "Paper Pandas and Jumping Frogs," published by China Books, San Francisco; 81 (t) & 81 (b) Nancy Palubnaik/Palubniak Studios, Inc.; 82 International Folk Art Foundation Collections at the Museum of International Folk Art, Santa Fe., photographer: Michel Monteaux; 83 (t) Keith McLeod Fund and Helen S. Coolidge Fund Courtesy of Museum of Fine Arts, Boston; 84 David T. Vernon, Colter Bay Indian Arts Museum, NPS; 85 (t) Derek Washington/Bruce Coleman, Inc.; 86 (t) Francekevich/The Stock Market; 86 (b) Robert Clarke/Photo Researchers; 87 Andy Levin/Photo Researchers; 88 Alan Smith/Tony Stone Images; 89 (tl) Luis Castaneda/The Image Bank; 89 (tr) Steve Elmore/The Stock Market; 90 Salzburg Marionette Theater, Salzburg Austria; 91 (t) From the Girard Foundation Collection in the Museum of International Folk Art, a unit of the Museum of New Mexico; 92 Becky Crouch Patterson.

Unit 05:

Harcourt Brace & Company:

93, 97 (b), 99 (b), 105, 106 (l) 107 (t) & 111 (b) Weronica Ankarorn; 106 (r) 107 (b)Victoria Bowen.

Other

94 Margaret Bourke-White,Life Magazine c.1946/Time, Inc.; 95 UPI/Corbis-Bettmann; 96 (t) Kunio Owaki/The Stock Market NY; 96 (b) Photography Purchase Fund, 1957.130/The Art Institute of Chicago; 97 (t) Flip Schulke; 98 Evan Agostini/Liaison; 99 (t) & 99 (t)(inset) Photograph by David Finn; 100, 101(t), & 101 (b) Photographs by Peter Ziebel from "Greening the City Streets" by Barbara Huff. Photographs copyright (c)1990 by Peter Ziebel. Reprinted by permission of Clarion Books/Houghton Mifflin Co. All rights reserved; 102 t) & 102 (b) Our Lady of Guadalupe School, Houston, Texas; 103 Nancy Hoyt Belcher; 104 (t) Jeremy Whitaker; 104 (b) Michael S. Yamashita; 108 Adam Woolfitt/Woodfin Camp & Associates; 109 Robert Frerck/Odyssey Productions; 110 Adam Woolfitt/Woodfin Camp & Associates; 111(t) Adam Woolfitt/Woodfin Camp & Associates; 112 (t) Kunio Owaki/The Stock Market; 112 (b) Dick Durrance III/Woodfin Camp & Associates.

Unit 06:

Harcourt Brace & Company:

119 (b), 123 (b), 125 (b) 129 (b) & 133 Weronica Ankarorn.

Other:

114 The Art Institute of Chicago, A. James Speyer Memorial, UNR Industries in honor of James W. Alsdorf, Barbara Neff Smith and Solomon Byron Smith funds, 1989.385 overall. Photograph by Thomas Cinoman. Published with permission of Martin Puryear; 116 photo © Descharnes & Descharnes Sarl; 117 Menil Foundation, Houston, Texas/Lauros-Giraudon, Paris/Superstock; 118 David Hockney #1 U.S. Trust/photo, Tyler Graphics LTD.; 119 (t) The Museum of Contemporary Art, Los Angeles. The Rita and Taft Schreiber Collection. Photo, Fredrik Nilsen; 120 Phil Taplin; 121 (t) Tia Magalon, School of Visual Arts, New York; 121 (bl) School of Visual Arts,New York; 121 (br) Tia